MW01703419

To William -
In the spirit of
Light and Love -
now and always -
Wayne

VOX

Valentino

ACROSS THE UNIVERSE

WAYNE VINCENT HATFORD

ISBN # 979-8-9860120-2-5

Whitley Heights Publishing
San Francisco, CA
www.valentinospeaks.com

Other Books by Wayne Vincent Hatford

Letters from Janice

Valentino Speaks

Going for Excelsior

Rudolph Valentino: The Untold Story

Beauty Wanted

Rudolph Valentino on the 2020's

Please visit www.valentinospeaks.com *for more information.*

ACKNOWLEDGMENTS

I'd like to thank those here present, those in spirit, those with whom I have lived and loved, those I have cared for, my companions, confidants, correspondents, for your love and support. ***Vi ringrazio di cuore***. (*I thank you from the bottom of my heart.*)

And especially to Rodolfo, ***gentilissimo sei***, (*how very kind you are*) - *he without whom none of our books would ever have been put to page. It's been my pleasure to work with you, to periodically cohabitate the ether for the purpose of communication.*

Offered in the spirit of love and service, I dedicate this book to Rudolph Valentino, movie star ***par excellence***, *purveyor of wit and wisdom, master metaphysician and all-around mensch.*

Wayne Vincent Hatford
San Francisco, California

Nota Bene (*P.S.*) *A special thanks to Shawn Schikora for his contributions to this project, also to Marcia Diefendorf for her assiduous and careful editing.*

Cover Design by Shelley Glasow @ goodlifeguide.com.

"There is something bigger and more worthwhile than the things we see about us, the things we live by and strive for. There is an undiscovered beauty, a divine excellence, just beyond us. Let us stand on tiptoe, forgetting the nearer things and grasp what we may."

Bernard Maybeck, Architect, 1923

MORCEAUX CHOISIS

(*Selected Bits*)

Rudolph Valentino invites you to consider each of the following topics, offered in no particular order, as stand-alones or one-offs in a series of concise essays. Some are esoteric, some descriptive, some practical. All are designed to stimulate thought for curiosity is the universal lubrication.

Like all of our collaborations, this anthology is channeled material - delivered to me via automatic writing. Any comments sourced from my consciousness alone are indicated as such by the use of italics. Everything else is Rodolfo. Words and phrases in other languages have been bolded and either translated or explained in context.

***Evviva la condivisione ed a Rodolfo, dico bravissimo**! (Here's to sharing, and to Rodolfo I say job well-done!)*

Fino alla prossima volta
(Until the next time)

Wayne Vincent Hatford

TABLE OF CONTENTS

1

QUADRANT

If you bisect a circle twice, each line equidistant to the other, you will have created four quadrants or right angles, also known as squares. Each square is a natural source of power given that two unequal or unregulated energies are at work, in conflict as it were, forming a dynamic with each other. As we have previously discussed, the focus is at the locus, the fulcrum where the two energies in question meet and have it out. That is the point where ideas are born, solutions to any dilemma.

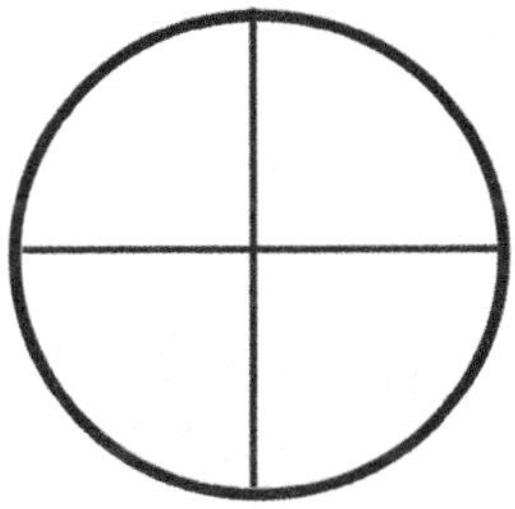

Now picture the arc that is created by drawing a quarter circle from the outer end of one axis of a quadrant to the outer end of another. Along this curvature lie your defenses and it is from there, energetically-speaking, that you can also go on the offensive by both making your presence known and offering solutions. That your line of defense/offense is arc-shaped tends to blunt any resistance you may encounter.

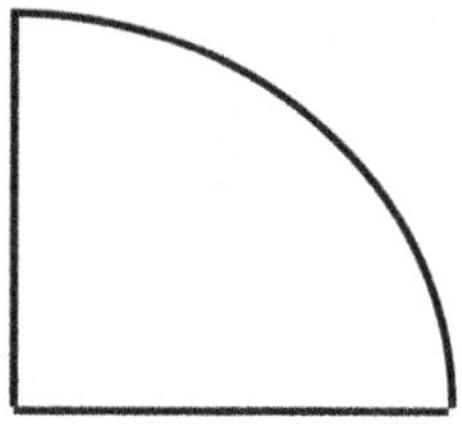

Sometimes fanning out is preferable to moving forward in a straight line as there is less drag and the possibility of more synergy and thrust: i.e. better efficiency. Here diffusion is the name of the game as opposed to a concentration of forces.

2

PLATONIC INTIMACY: THE ART OF AUTOMATIC WRITING

The following material is excerpted from our first joint effort, "Valentino Speaks," published in 2011.

"What is automatic writing? It is one of the methods that we in the Astral use to communicate with those who are in the flesh.

(*Speaking to the author*) Know that I cannot of my own free will make an automatic writing session with you occur. First, you have to be in agreement. Then we need technical support ~ those who hold the wires or in our case the silver cord that serves as a link between my thoughts and your writing. The technicians I speak of are, of course, skilled in this sort of transmission, aligning themselves with our energies and acting as conduits, helping to pass information from this dimension to yours. It is quite a feat! Your "H" (*making reference to my paternal grandmother, Alice Vincent Hatford*) is the prime holder of this font of energy ~ to be used in all of our communications. I am very grateful to her and her colleagues for all of their help and assistance. I know that you are too. They are the ones who generate and hold the necessary space so that I can communicate with you in this manner.

To effect this means of communication, we on this side have first to find and then wrestle with a ripple in the space and time continuum. Once achieved, we conduct energy through the Veil and down a focus chute, working as a unit. All this must occur sequentially as well as concurrently in order for my thoughts to be able to connect with the tip of the pen in your hand.

The energy used to channel is like tension in a wound-up clock spring, completely available until all of a sudden there's no more torque. As a result, every automatic writing session has a shelf life, able to last for only a certain amount of time."

Postscript, received in 2023

If you have written with me, you have lived with me.

Whenever there is interdimensional communication, platonic intimacy occurs. Indeed, it is always part of the equation. Automatic writing, usually done in cursive then transcribed to print, documents both the experience and information imparted.

In using this term I do not speak of a relationship per se, as defined by Earth Realm standards. Rather, it is a temporary congruency and in a sense such interactions are even more intimate than physical ones because in order to effectuate this process both parties must enter into each other's energetic spaces and temporarily blend their respective intellects and prowesses, creating adjoining lanes on the information highway. Channeling is akin to living together, being domiciled under the same roof. This is one of the most dynamic interactions possible because there are no hidden corners and everything is on the table. Mutually and respectively we are open books.

3

PANUM

Nourishment is wanted and nourishment there shall be, in every aspect of incarnated and spiritual life. The concept is the same, the functions as well. In Spanish, one says "**nos da de comer**" (*it feeds us/gives us something to eat.*) In this instance we shall consider the Latin word for bread to fill that bill, the title of this set of reflections.

Panum is sustenance without which none of us can exist, neither you in the body or me in spirit. All of us require replenishment and this is what **panum** supplies.

What, more specifically, is **panum?** Prayer/Thought/Love/Hope - any and all expressions of goodness; these help nourish the soul. What, on my side of the Veil, nourishes the soul? One-ness, Light and Love, for without these ingredients no spirit can ever be at peace.

Panum as a concept is transmigratory, therefore equally important in either dimension. We also inhale it into the body via air and then exhale it etherically.

In and out we breathe. In either case this, again, is **panum.**

4

CLOACA MAXIMA

"The deepest and grimmest impression of antiquity I have ever received." ~ Henry James

He was speaking about Rome's famous sewer system, a marvel of its age which it continues to be ~ throughout the centuries, in James' time and to the present. Romans viewed the movement of water as sacred, and so it was in any application, including the movement of waste in order to provide a better quality of life for all of Rome's citizens. How to define waste in our personal realm? Primarily thought, those that are toxic or in some way malevolent, those that limit or inhibit rather than expand, those that in and of themselves present as radioactive because in a sense they are, those that turn upon being destructive or lead to deprivation, those that in their essence do not nourish the soul. There are many forms of waste and some of the most injurious are the ones that are self-created. Sure, our environments can also contain waste and in this century they often do, what you call pollution. That said, it is easier to be aware of one's surroundings than one's quality of thought. The errant ones do often slip by, almost without notice.

Ye must catch yourselves thinking, more often than not, in order to correct this very human tendency which is not only to mull things over but to chew on spurious thoughts. **Bagatelles,** (*trifles*) the French call them, also **lubies** (*whims.*) Neither is very productive. I spoke about imaging in our most recent tome ("*Rudolph Valentino on the 2020's" - page 66.*) This is perhaps the most creative form of thought, and the very best use of your brain power. The entity Abraham, who many of you know has been given voice by Esther Hicks, says, over and over again, "Go for a better thought." It cannot be repeated enough that this is a technique to flush your personal sewer - to clear your mind, cleansing it of dross. One's own **cloaca maxima** must flow without impediment in order for us to be our most productive selves.

What are the consequences of a chokehold on the flow? A diminution, a narrowing, myopia that results in an excess of navel-gazing. And the worst kind of intolerance occurs when we turn it upon ourselves. You have a friend (*speaking to the author*) who wonders if moping has a purpose. It does in the sense that upon having become immersed in that state of affairs much work is required to achieve emancipation. To mope is to be fogbound which speaks of limitation. Therefore it is not a constructive pursuit and when you can name the behavior, meaning that you are consciously aware of having dived into that pool, it is providential to get out of it as soon as you can. The "mope" is akin to swimming in a sewer where effluents and malodors are sure to hold sway. It is often characterized by loss of interest or a sense of incongruence, i.e. feeling that you and your environment are not in synch.

The human entity is a self-charging battery always in the process of amping up or running down, a consistent and constant phenomenon. Moping, similar to being listless, has the effect of draining one's batteries to the extent that initiating a recharge becomes more and more difficult. To mope, therefore, is to grope in the dark. Whenever moping appears to be the flavor of the day, an intervention is called for which again is to think a better thought ~ as much or as often as you can. This restores flow, personal power, and equilibrium between input and output.

Energetically-speaking, moping is akin to powering down without turning off the switch.

5

DETRITUS

"Rock in small particles or other material worn or broken away from a mass, as by the action of water or glacial ice; any disintegrated material; debris."

The experience of aging, whether brief or prolonged, has a scouring effect upon the human body. Indeed, we continually shed: skin, hair, fluids and waste, all manner of personal detritus or debris.

And likewise does a soul become scoured during the course of an incarnation, those barbs or spurs we were born to reckon with ultimately smoothed and polished, or hopefully so. The action of water is the emollient, symbolically, and often actually, to effectuate this result.

One speaks of washing away sins. I would describe it differently. I speak not of sin which is a man-made contention but rather of a determination on the part of the soul to self-regulate, specifically to curate, triage certain aspects of self, those traits or tendencies that you have determined need attention prior to inhabiting a human form which is to say entering a specific incarnation. This process will, as a matter of course, produce detritus, sometimes a lot of it. Much of the human experience is about letting go, realizing that you cannot hang on to everything, including questionable proclivities, questionable to yourself and sometimes to the society you inhabit as well.

Why are we in the body? Is there such a thing as perfection? Will we ever trim ourselves, our authentic selves, to the nub or core?

There is no such thing as perfection but balance is what we can and will achieve, the ultimate goal of each individual soul.

Every human being is like a spinning top, electrons constantly in motion ~ and the fewer obtuse angles, the fewer appendages, the smoother the spin. This is the essence of balance. Unregulated energies are the by-product of unwarranted appendages, singular or plural, individual or corporate.

6

RHYTHM & BEAT

For without one we cannot have the other. Helix-like, they are entwined.

We often associate rhythm with dance, beat as well. That is definitely an arena where they are noticed and thought of as a gift. Indeed, those who wholeheartedly embrace them tend to be widely praised in the performing arts. What is perhaps less known or realized is that each human being is in possession of his or her own particular rhythm. Yes, my rhythms are different from yours **et ainsi de suite** (*and so it goes.*) Likewise beat which, as already stated, cannot be separated from rhythm.

Rhythm and beat, combined, are akin to percolation, effervescence, permeation. Together they create a signature, your own personal whiff. I allude here to smell, but one's signature extends to all the senses and it is continually exuded, therefore noted by your fellow men and women in every encounter.

As the definition states, this was the time of year when France was rife with fog, and indeed the French revolution was foggy, prone to excess. How is that any different from life as we know it in 2024? It's almost like this era is a doppelgänger for the final quarter of the 18th century. We walk in fog yet we must trust in ourselves and our fellow men and women to get where we are going. Surely there will be some stumbles but keep an eye out for candles, those sparks of Light and Life that are ever present.

I wanted to inject a bit of history here because today's stories are so similar; actually, they are reflexive. Where are we on the pendulum swing? And can it be brought to bear on current events? Strange times when lies become truths in the minds of men ~ yet all of you have the ability to discern, to separate the wheat from the chaff. **Mes amis, réfléchissez bien avant d'agir; soyez prudents!** (*My friends, reflect before taking action; be careful!*)

8

GORDIAN KNOT

In Greek legend, a complicated knot, tied by King Gordius of Phrygia, that Alexander the Great cut with a sword; a complicated and intricate problem.

What it appears society is in the midst of.

How many people say they are being hindered or constrained? How many feel tied to one place or robot-like courses of action? How many feel stifled by some unknown force, theory or thought? This is the time to cut that knot, the symbolic and yet very real knot we are all engaged with (we, meaning Earth Plane residents.) The Gordian knot can only be untied by you, the collective you ~ those who see Light, Truth and the actual pursuit of happiness. No false equivalents need apply.

It is said that a Gordian knot cannot be undone. Of course it can, and so it is written that these years, the current ones, are when mankind unties it and/or each individual cuts him/her self loose. Again, it can be done. We tie ourselves in knots over all kinds of situations. Why not reverse that tendency? The urge to be free prevails and so shall it be.

9

PICCOLE SQUADRATURE

(*Small Square Shapes*)

The value of the **scatto** or snap ~ which is to say a moment in time.

What in the world is he talking about? Picture-taking and the resulting photos which are composed of small squares, sometimes rectangles as well. One could also say that oil paintings and other works of art are in the same ballpark. They, too, are **piccole squadrature**.

In order to best understand this topic, consider your cell phones and computer screens. Like cameras, they capture moments, both singular and plural. And the plural ones are often in the form of videos, having various lengths. Since the beginning of time, mankind has been thinking about moments, isolated visions that stand out as compared to all the others.

And this is what you see, the function of the eyes. They continually take innumerable individual snaps, **scatti**, **piccole**

squadrature, that capture specific moments. However, the eyes are designed to continually record visual impressions in a stream of consciousness sort of way, so isolating a moment can be challenging. Artists do it when they choose a subject. Other people do it by utilizing devices that isolate a second or less, delivering an image.

Even if we were bereft of technologies, it would still be possible to catch an image and mentally hold on to it. All human beings are capable of registering images on the mind's eye which is markedly different from its physical counterparts. That said, one must see before anything can be. Visualization is key to making things happen.

10

BRUCIABILE

(*Burnable*)

This term relates to fire, perhaps the most important element in the sense that it produces the most visual cues and/or effects. Inherent in any fire are flames. Flame is the single event, the focus of transfiguration, transformation. What is not burnable, one could say, is obviously not prima facie material. What is burnable is everything else. In every flame there lies hope; in every flame there lies change. Fires or flames are a means to radically change, rearrange the molecules of any thing or any environment, literally of course but also figuratively.

The Earth was once far more flaming than it currently is yet the Sun reminds us of flame. So does the temperature rise so prevalent now and soon to become even more relevant. I also want to speak of fire more allegorically, of flame, because those images are also associated with Love. Have you ever heard tell of a flaming kiss? It is with the ardor of Love that consciousnesses are entwined, that souls link for complimentary experiences. Love is also represented by flame, let me say eternal.

What do we not want to burn down? What do we want to reform? Does something have to be burnable to be real? These are questions to be pondered, reflected upon.

In the meantime, never underestimate the power of a single flame!

11

GLI SGUARDI

(*Gazes*)

This is quite personal as I was accused of having a rather magnetic **sguardo**. Actually it is a reflection. When one human being sets their gaze upon another there is a mirror-like opportunity for the second individual to see themselves reflected in said gaze - the initial stage of a gazer/gazee interaction. Then roles switch and the resulting energy flow can be like a mini **coup de foudre**, ("*love at first sight*" *or the promise of it*) akin to a lightning bolt.

What, then, is a **sguardo**? It is an instance where one or another reveals his or her soul to the object of their affection. This **sguardo** moment is often a precursor to falling in love although that is not a requisite outcome. Sometimes the glances exchanged are all about appreciation and recognition of each other's soul energy. Sometimes, too, they can be exciting, an impulse to get to know the other person better, sexually explore, or both.

Sguardi are one of the kindest expressions those in the flesh can ever offer one another.

12

LO SCHERMO

(*Movie Screen*)

Some posit that the world we inhabit (again, the 'we' refers to the more than me) is a two dimensional experience that only looks like it's a three. The movie screen, therefore, is perfectly analogous. It is in essence flat yet what is projected upon it appears to have depth and dimension.

Well, **mes amis**, you get to project whatever you will. **Lo schermo** is simply a tool for playing in this realm, or rather your realm. What you project is totally of your own invention, your own guise. Such fun to play with reality, to imagine the imaginable, also the unimaginable as that, too, is an option and what artists and inventors often do.

I straddled the first days of cinema and its later projections. My era was short (*the heyday of silent film*), yet it inspired others to think beyond the "dumb show" (*Mime, also an allusion to Shakespeare*).

When, by the way, are you not looking at screens in **anno domini** 2024? They are more of a conscious aspect of life than ever before and, the possibilities are endless.

13

JOHN SINGER SARGENT

I knew him not during our respective incarnations which overlapped yet I knew him by virtue of his work and reputation. And I also knew him because of his affinity with Italy and the luster of his art.

Signor Sargent: his eye for beauty has never dimmed nor will it ever.

He is a study in the beneficence of Light. All of his paintings and watercolors are infused with it and his drawings literally jump off the page, often with only a minimum of lines. Sargent was able to be "at one" with his settings, whether nature-inspired or architectural, as well as with his sitters, those he captured on canvas. Some artists focus on soul, some on the personality. Sargent was able to convey both, the soul of his subject and the personality **du jour**, in every portrait he painted.

You may wonder why he came to be included in this book. He is, if you will, the consummate creative. Not only was he able to portray beauty on canvas and paper, his life was such that he enveloped himself in it, socially and professionally. And he was prolific in his work, generous in his knowledge of the world. Born in Italy to American parents, he lived the life of an international, savoring beauty wherever he found it. He was also a linguist, able to write and converse fluently in several languages.

John's work is timeless. I honor his dedication and his ability to convey his art in ways that can easily be comprehended by the majority of people who view it. Sargent is in a class of his own and he straddled eras, as do you my **plume** (*feather, with the implication of scribe ~ speaking to the author.*) He hobnobbed with the hoi polloi and patricians of his own generation, those before and those beyond as well.

John Singer Sargent: a purveyor of beauty who never ceases to inspire and amaze.

14

ERGO, EGO

Once an entity is possessed of a physical shape, which is to say that he or she has entered the physical world, it almost goes without saying that the ego has also been born or rather re-awakened. For the ego was chosen, is chosen, prior to inception. Picture, if you will, a **grand magasin** (*department store*) possessing every possible variety of ego ingredients. Strands of DNA could be another representation of this concept. Well, once combined or woven it is intangible until it's not. A baby is born with its ego intact.

What is ego? Sense of self is the basic definition. It is also a large part of one's personality or human experience. So you do not develop an ego as you mature; rather, it is fully formed although not yet fully expressed when a baby exits the birth canal. This aspect is thusly gifted because being on the Earth Plane necessitates having an ego; actually you could not function in this setting without one.

What is the purpose of ego? It cocoons us; it soothes us. And it does shape-shift as well due to pushback and experiences as they occur. Egos do get adjusted from time to time but during the course of an incarnation they never intrinsically change.

15

CODE

A mysterious concept if ever there was one. Secrecy is implied, or opaqueness. However, all matter is subject to code, therefore to some sort of programming. This is expressed in many different ways, and according to the needs of those who invent them.

There are genetic codes, to be sure, furthermore others of the more mathematical variety. Code in one respect can be related to the previous topic, ego. The ego is a formulation of code as are the cells of one's body ~ based theoretically on those who have gone before us, ethnically and spiritually. Then there are codes for everything else, what in your world are sometimes referred to as algorithms: codes that make things work, codes that unlock power, codes that heal genes, codes that make space travel a reality.

We live in a coded world, my friends, and I am speaking of the one we perceive whatever our place, be it physical, what you perceive, or astral, what I know.

16

THINGS VERSUS FEELINGS

We perceive things as solid or real, which they are in this environment, but also keep in mind that they are composed of molecules which have electrons and which also accommodate some space between them. So what appears to be solid actually is not - in process or in a process, as are we all. You could say the same about a physical body as you could a rock. Both are continually in process, in a metamorphosis of some kind. All this is to say that 'things' have less import than we think they do.

What about feelings? Here is the major difference: every feeling is registered upon the spiritual apparatus. I use this term to reference beyond the physical body or, rather, one's motherboard. Earth Plane residents consider feelings to be intangible, therefore not nearly as important as things and/or the amassing of them. But, **mes amis**, because your feelings are registered on your etheric body, they go with you; they are with you, always. No money, jewels or works of art can transgress the dimensions. However, feelings can. Feelings are part of our overall learning experiences, the intangible tangibles. Indeed, they are the residue of every thought and/or action taken while inhabiting a body, or shall we say the physical vehicle.

Do not minimize your feelings. But don't maximalize them either. Each is to be savored in a natural way and savoring is the key; drowning in them is not. As is true in all circumstances, a certain balance must be maintained in order to have an optimal living experience, whatever the game, whatever the plane.

Postscript:

Earth Plane thinking tends to focus on value and things have value ~ as compared to feelings which are often considered an afterthought or by-product.

During one's life review, post-transition, you look at what made the most feeling impact, not at your material conquests which are and were irrelevant. What did you do? And how did you feel about it?

17

TIMELINES

A timeline is a frame of reference, a spine upon which to hang one's experiences. Are they linear and do they overlap, entwine or perhaps zigzag? Let us dig in, but first here are some thoughts I previously shared that are germane to this topic.

(*The following two quotes are excerpted from "Valentino Speaks" ~ published in 2011.*)

"Time's mission is to keep us in the present. But how, you ask? By providing us with a false sense of the past and a shadow impression of the future, in other words, by constantly reminding us that all we really have is right here, right now ~ in the moment."

"The past and future can only be referenced in the present. Why? Because all events are simultaneous, the only difference being that each one functions within a specific vibration and therefore can only be seen, felt and experienced when we and that event are in sync."

In a way his-story, or her-story, is the study of timelines, the threads of which form the basis for our perceptions of reality.

Pick any point on a random timeline and there will be an infinite number of other timelines that could intersect with it, 'could' being the operative word, interlacing and interlocking, intertwining as well. Every second of any twenty four hour period is an opportunity to veer to an alternate timeline, should we so choose.

Your interlocutor wonders if timelines are extant in the non-corporeal world (*speaking to the author.*) In other words, do timelines have a role in the Astral experience? No, **messieurs/dames**, they do not. Their existence is known, of course, but such frames of reference and their attendant effects are null and void. The only way timelines come into play is a matter of choice, applicable to a disincarnate when he or she re-launches, known to you as the moment of birth. Upon being born you will have injected yourself into an overall timeline from which other timelines protrude and of which you may partake whenever you so desire.

In essence then, timelines are an element of Earth-based reality and are perpetuated solely as a device upon which to hang our hats while basking in body consciousness.

Any timeline is rife with possibility and that is what makes each one so exciting. You see, you often take detours, try out this timeline or that one to see how it fits (or doesn't fit) for we are not tied to any, whether in the waking state or dream world. Entering or exiting a time line is solely at our discretion. Now each incarnation and its unfurling have a probable timeline, overall, as I have already stated, but detours should be and often are welcome. Explorations of timelines are as simple as reading books. And if on the street you suddenly decide to turn left instead of going right that, too, is a deviation to another timeline. You see, quite subtle they can be!

18

NOSTALGIA/LONELINESS

Two Sides of the Same Coin

There is no consistent formula for a constructive stint in physical form, what you know of as an individual incarnation or internship in the ways of the flesh.

It has come to my attention that this is a duality that wants to be addressed. What do we get out of wrapping our arms around one versus the other? Or, are they a package, meaning you can't immerse yourself in one without the other?

Both of these states of being have their drawbacks or rather cautionary tales. Getting too involved in the one or the other removes us from the stream of life and, artificially so, at least in terms of consciousness. Loneliness, especially, is a trap from which exits can be rare. Falling into it or regaling yourself with sad stories of lack of support or even touch may be appealing to one's personality but not at all conducive to spiritual health and well-being. Stuck-ness, I call it, stubborn, too. Clinging to loneliness is both unattractive and condescending, condescending because you are never alone. 'You' is always with you, first and foremost. Then, too, there are your spirit guides, invisible to the eye perhaps, but ever-present.

Loneliness does not comport with that truth, not at all. What is the key to dispelling such self-induced propaganda? Interest, attention, spark, all of which are self-generated and that's the way things always work, no matter who else may be present in your sphere. In the final analysis every move you make is the result of a self catalyzation. Others may inspire you but they can do nothing for you. You must 'do' for yourself.

Nostalgia, on the other hand, is far less toxic and therefore grates less upon well-being. But what you may remember as being quite idyllic perhaps never really was. So again while it may be comforting to go there it is not viable to stay in that space too long. Fleeting is the best approach to nostalgia; keep it fleeting, because it is. Being too attached to past practice or events is counterproductive and an exercise in futility.

Surely you may say, "Rudy, did you not partake in nostalgic activities?" In some, yes, but mostly in film roles and a bit in my home space too. Playing dress-up is a form of nostalgia and that aspect of it can be fun, also informative and relevant to the soul's experience.

19

BIRTHING

You will note a verb form here rather than a noun. That is because it is a process, not achieved only at the moment of birth, meaning the first inhale/exhale. Much of what happens in preparation for a birth remains a mystery and so it must but I can divulge certain aspects, speaking in general.

As you may imagine it is quite personal, therefore "different" for each soul, upon each entrance to each incarnation. I have spoken about choosing an overall time line. That, of course, takes place, and then the soul in question must also know what aspects or issues they would like to conceive, and by that I mean bring into being. We create all of our issues based on pieces of code prior to joining with the new vehicle, mother and the family circle to be. They can only flower, however, while in the body.

One cannot say how much time is involved in all of these preparations because the function of time applies not. The Spirit World does not reference time, ever. And no soul or spirit, because they are the same, ever enters into any agreement under duress. They are ready to enter the flesh when they are born and have indeed prepared themselves to do so.

Some pregnancies do not come to term, however, and that is not a tragedy just a reflection of the experiences those involved wanted to create. In Earth time a pregnancy takes nine months, an interesting number because it is emblematic of completion. But for 'the baby to be' time does not exist and consciousness makes the leap immediately, does not gestate or percolate in order to become fuller. It is instantaneous, in a union with the mother for temporary accommodation.

Do entities/souls/spirits celebrate when one of their **proches** (*close relatives or friends*) enters the physical realm? There are loving gestures, to be sure. More than that, it's a knowing that all is right, all will be well.

20

MIDDLE NAMES

One's primary names, first and last, combine to create a sound signature that is unique for every individual. These are the names by which you are most commonly known and therefore how you are likely to be addressed in the Public Square. Name is also game; it provides the people you meet with an idea of who you are. You are a visual, your physical self, and you are a vibration, your spiritual self. Names flesh things out in that they create a sound that relates to your presence which also provides additional information to those you meet and those who know of you.

You (*speaking to the author*) have a middle name that links you to the family of your paternal grandmother, Alice Vincent Hatford. The middle name, for those who have them, adds nuance to the first and last and further refines the sound signature created by uttering it aloud or hearing it in the mind while seeing it on paper. Your middle name adds refinement and perhaps a touch of the old World, given those particular ancestors who can be traced back to France.

I, on the other hand, was blessed with a number of middle names, some of which connect me with my mother's blood line and others with my father's family. Rodolfo Alfonso Raffaello Pierre Filibert Guglielmi di Valentina d'Antonguella is my moniker, and quite a mouthful, **n'est-ce pas**? (*Isn't it?*) In my youth I was known as Rodolfo Guglielmi yet I was drawn to the 'titled' portion of my name, indicated by the use of the word '**di**' (*from or of.*) Di Valentina d'Antonguella became Valentino and there you have it, my **nom de plume** or **nom de travail** ~ how I was known in the world once my star began to rise.

That I fiddled with my name did not change it; instead, what I did was to claim it ~ in a slightly different way. My suite of names gave me latitude, emphasized my pulchritude, contributed to my success and enabled me to play many roles. In my case, fluidity was a great asset.

In the Western World, people usually have one middle name yet in Europe one could have many. And one can also have none. The first and last are sufficient, but middle names add color, sometimes heft as well. Stylistically speaking we float on our names so you could also say they are our cloud-markers, emblematic of the physical space we occupy. Furthermore, names have the function of a **stemma** (*coat of arms*) which links us to those who have gone before, our family trees.

21

THE CANVAS UPON WHICH WE PAINT

Body-bound Sojourns

These are synonyms for life as you know it, the doing and the being of it all. There is so much more, of course, indeed a plethora, but let us confine ourselves to the Earth Plane in this discussion.

(*Rudy, quoting himself.*) ~ "Women are not in love with me, but with the picture of me on the screen. I am merely the canvas on which women paint their dreams."

Here I am referring to projection, my self, or rather the body I once wore, as a figment of mass consciousness, adored by many and hated by some as well. One's stirrings on the pathways of life always make waves, how could they not?

As part of our agreement with our 'self' to temporarily become body-bound, we are each provided with a canvas, a screen on which to paint our dreams. Some of them veer to the concrete ~ reflecting our proclivities, the things and situations we would like to manifest. Others are musings, projections, if you will, such as ideals of perfection, flights of fancy and the like. All are valid.

The canvas upon which we paint may be used however you wish but this I ask you to consider: how not to waste your powers of persuasion on specters ~ which are usually based on the fear of something that might happen. When you put a lot of energy into fearing a possibility, you may unwittingly become the source of its manifestation.

Creating what you really want requires being assiduous in your thinking, for as you think so shall it be. It is akin to an artist wielding his brush with care and foresight.

Some people choose to see negativity lurking around every corner. I humbly suggest that you do not.

22

EIGHTY IS WEIGHTY

Being an Elder

The trajectory of my life was short by all commonly held standards. And I am speaking of course of the 'I' who is here present, who you have come to know as Rodolfo Valentino. I am he; he is me. And I have also been other people, held spaces and consciousness, in other times and places ~ as have all of you, **mes amis**. Life is a rondel where we each get to play different parts. As Rodolfo many of mine were on the silver screen but there were plenty of others to portray as well. One part I never got to play, however, is that of an elder ~ except while wearing make-up in my final film.

Some argue that age 84 is the magic number in terms of having had a full life. This is because the planet Uranus requires that amount of time to return to its point of origin, having traversed the full 360 degrees of the Zodiac. Uranus is the planet of surprises and you may have noticed yours are on the upswing (*speaking to the author.*)

(*I do happen to be 80 during the writing of this book.*)

Yes, eighty can be weighty ~ if only for the number of years one is carrying. But, does it need to be? By the way, a 'full life' has many numbers; I completed what I needed to in 31, what I had contracted with myself to accomplish. You (*speaking to the author*) have had friends who left as early as 21, **scomparsi** (*the Italian euphemism for dead.*) They, too, had full lives. Each of you has your own special timeline, the length of which is still to be determined. Why? Incarnated life is flexible as are timelines.

Edith Wharton ~ "There are two ways of spreading light: to be the candle or the mirror that reflects it."

In terms of being an elder, regardless of chronological age, Mrs. Wharton had it right. Age is a number doted upon by doctors, not a true reflection of one's state of being or wisdom. If there is any formula for the best and highest use of your time while on the Earth Plane, this is it! Light is ours to spread, and so we shall.

23

INTERNAL ORGANS

Not the flesh and blood kind but rather relating to your inner fugues. Also known as the space within a space, background music, the place from which you operate. In the dictionary of life, they are emblematic of our eternal chords.

There are two primary aspects to a fugue. One has to do with music and I would argue that we each dance to our own tune, listen to our own rhythms, treble and bass, all the time. The other relates to consciousness and how we choose to focus it.

1. "A musical composition for a definite number of parts or voices, in which a subject is announced in one voice, imitated in succession by each of the other voices, and developed contrapuntally."

2. "A state of psychological amnesia during which the subject seems to behave in a conscious and rational way, but, upon return to normal consciousness, cannot remember the period of time nor what he or she did during it."

Der Hauptbahnhof (*the main railroad station*) ~ from which all trains depart and return is known in bodily terms as the heart. Symbolically it is the conductor of your internal symphony and coordinator of the "all that is" in the mini universe of each incarnated self. It is also where you can immerse yourself in order to become better attuned. So the bits of being un-focused we all experience from time to time are synonymous with checking-in. Both definitions of fugue are always operable and fully in effect.

You may also compare one's internal symphony with the sounds church organs make. Inherent in that are stirrings and certain elements of drama. Indeed, organ music is often associated with spiritual matters, providing us with moments to pause and reflect.

That said, there is no one who needs an external source to spark either of these aforementioned conventions. The joy is in the fact that they are entirely self-generated even if, and/or when, you think they are not.

24

ASTRAL VOYAGING

Dream Life

At Rodolfo's behest, I am including three quotes from "Valentino Speaks" © 2011 that pertain to this topic. You will also find an addendum below, material received in 2023.

"Dreams give us endless opportunities to exercise our creativity. Indeed, upon entering the dream state each night we become expert actors, writers, set and costume designers, ready to ply our trade. Our dreams can never be too incongruous by the way. It's only in the light of day that they seem to be. Dreams also tend to highlight issues that, for one reason or another, have been submerged. As we dream, we get to dislodge them from their moorings so that they can rise to the surface and be noticed, sort of like cream in unprocessed milk. Even though they may sometimes be convoluted, our dreams give us a chance to experiment, unfettered by what is commonly thought of as waking reality."

"Dreaming is about you experiencing you, beyond the limitations of so-called waking life. In many ways dreams are like home shopping catalogues. In them we get to try on feelings as well as accomplish things that might seem to us as out of the ordinary. Dreams are guides for 'ways to be' ~ vehicles for more fully rounding out our life experiences."

"In the vastness of Universal Intelligence dreams were devised as a conveyance, showcasing our issues by night and then, with the dawning of the next day, giving us an opportunity to make them part of our waking consciousness. In the aggregate, dreams are thematic propositions presented in fragmented ways, often defying logic but usually rather brilliantly developed. All dreams have rhyme and reason. It behooves us, therefore, to try to capture their essential meanings. Again, when examining a dream, pay attention to the feelings that have been evoked rather than thinking about literal interpretations. Therein lies the truth."

Addendum

Let us focus on the dreams that occur when we lose consciousness which is typically at night. Why do they happen some nights as opposed to others?

There is never a time when dreams do not take place as this is part and parcel of journeying in the Astral. It's just that some of them remain submerged, not rising to the surface of conscious thought. So dreams are frequently disjointed and sometimes they also address deep-seated fears. And even the ones that make you feel uneasy have merit as they signal short circuits in your overall web or motherboard. Dreams are opportunities to deal with your own set of cards ~ in a direct way without the filter of personality.

We go to the Astral each night or when taking a daytime nap so as not to lose touch. We are grounded in the Earth Plane yet we must also remain comfortable in the abode we will inhabit after death.

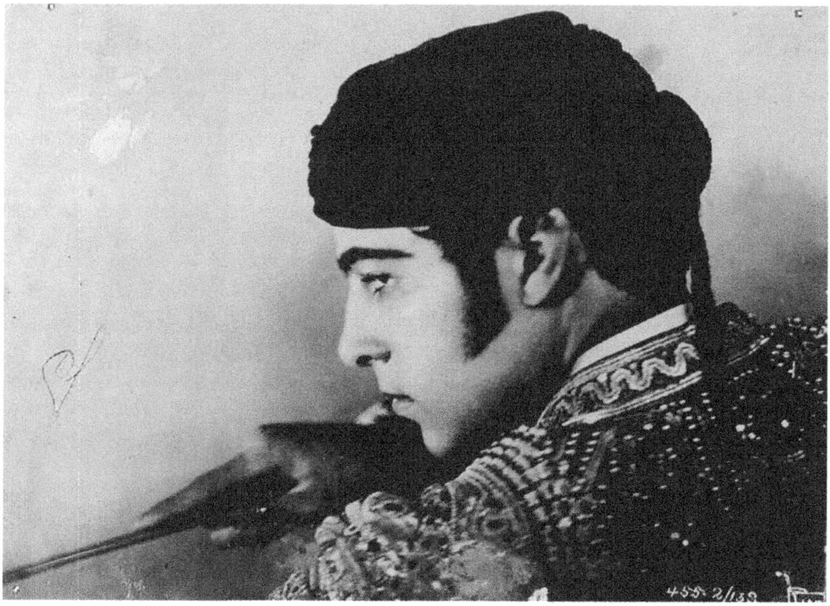

25

TODAY'S HOLLYWOOD

Question: Working in Hollywood today what roles would you choose to play? Would you also produce or direct films?

This is a hypothetical but I am pleased to answer your questions. Know that I can never re-gather the molecules that once formed the body of Rudolph Valentino nor can I breathe air into his lungs. I can use that essence, however, create its etheric form at will, as that is never lost. I come to you as Rodolfo because this is how you would know me and this is how I am. I am and have also been many other personalities, inhabited many other bodies, during the course of eternity as have you. So if I were to re-assemble Rudy into flesh and bone what would I want to be doing in Hollywood?

Given that I could have that body again and be the same age as when I died, I would want to become a character actor, immerse myself in those parts ~ even consciously decide to be ugly if a role calls for it. I only touched on that by playing my older self in "Son of the Sheik." And I would want to direct as well, to have an artistic vision and then bring it to fruition with all the accompanying details. The other aspects of movie-making I think, at least for my purposes, would remain in other hands.

I hope this answer is clear and will quench your thirst as to what I might or could do should I have another run at the Rodolfo corpus mentis.

26

ASTRAL RESIDENCIES

Upon death the door swings open and here I am speaking allegorically. The lines get blurred and/or just a bit fuzzy as to you all shall be possible. Now you probably don't figure that out immediately, at least I did not. But it soon becomes clear that 'as you think so shall it be' has suddenly become the rule rather than the exception. And there is no lag time. You may create any environment you choose; you may also flip through your own catalogue (again I speak allegorically) and choose any number of personal stats or aspects from any number of personalities you have lived and known, any combination you want, sort of like trying on endless numbers of outfits, mix and match. These become your new guise, subject of course to change.

Some people wonder if there are any rules in the new 'home' dimension. There are some, and they vary according to each individual energy signature and how its arrival is perceived by the living, breathing entity that is the essence of the Astral Plane. This is not a person but, as you would understand it, a matrix or energy grid where Intelligence reigns. And the most wonderful thing about your new home is that in it you can endlessly explore the 'you that is you' as well as all of its components and/or potential components, what you may call aspects of personality. You can try them on for size during your Astral residency and therefore, if you want, prepare to use some, none or all in the next incarnation ~ for each time we are re-born into human form we wear a different guise, what you perceive to be a fully-formed personality.

Post death is a happy time for all who come that way and that is, of course, all of you because death is an 'all' encompassing experience. For each of you the crossing will be different, the traversing of dimensional lines, according to and because of the beliefs you hold. So there is 'no one size fits all' in the matter of death. Let me say, however, that Light is ever-present in this process and if you allow yourself to be bathed in it your passage will be smooth, your adjustment to the new life as well.

Some also wonder if there are any measures for how long a soul may reside elsewhere, i.e. non-corporeally. No, again it is a completely individualized experience and based on choice or rather a series of choices.

27

ANGELS & SPIRIT GUIDES

You already know that everyone has them and indeed the latter is a position one might readily assume during their astral residency. However, so many factors are at play as to whether or not that will be the case because there has to be alignment between you and your incarnated 'brother/sister.'

We have many astral stays and I cannot put a number on them except to say a plural is involved. Rare is the individual who does not choose this vocation at some time and here again I am speaking of Spirit Guides.

Angels, conceptually, have a fiercer spin to their vibration and represent, therefore, in those **deus ex machina** happenings when it seems that miracles occur. Actually miracles do occur because Angels can tweak probabilities when it is not time for a soul to pass (saved by the bell), as often there will be a sound associated with the event or the incarnate will hear some kind of music.

Spirit Guides, on the other hand, are known to whisper in your ear to give you alternatives or ideas to consider. You, however, always have the last say. One of the most important things to understand is that each soul is autonomous, therefore owner of all their decisions.

Angels are the backstop and they only intervene in moments of great crisis when a detour is required, actually requested, subliminally if you will, of the Higher Self. Both of these roles are beautiful and each and every human being can be grateful that this is so.

Uplifting and enlightening, these are the verbs that apply to all of their work.

28

CHARACTERS

Screen, Stage & Print

Do they live? Are they akin to flesh and blood counterparts? Are screen characters any different from those chosen to populate a book?

Characters which are born of the human mind do possess a certain amount of energy, force if you will, especially if they are innately dramatic, but do they also exist on other timelines which may indeed be the question? No, they do not. They have been given a life in order to advance a plot yet they breathe not, are not the same as your human selves. They do, however, also have an energy signature, some of which seem to live on forever. Take some of my screen adventures, or rather consider them. The archetype that survives my career is that of the Sheik. He is me, at least in the eyes of my current day fans, especially those who are the most ardent. So you could say "He lives."

Some characters are only alive for the run of a play or the length of a film or until the final page of a novel. And then there are the rarer ones who do appear to have a life of their own, the key word being 'appear.' They only appear to live on because something about them strikes a universal chord, having the effect of affixing said character upon the whole of mass consciousness. Some of Shakespeare's characters are thusly remembered, Falstaff, for example, also Romeo and Juliet.

29

NEW AGE

In today's world a two word phrase that's often bandied about. So what, exactly, is its import? And how might it affect our general bandwidth?

The key part of this expression is 'age' of which Planet Earth has had many. Indeed, they come and they go with great regularity in the form of millennia, specifically two or in pairs. Indeed, every two thousand years a different element begins its reign, signaling a change in the overall flavor of the affairs of mankind. And as there are only four: fire, water, air, and earth, we have already seen repeats. Yes, these general influences repeat but never the details. How each element shift manifests is a reflection of the consciousness of those experiencing it, hence different every time.

We have, of late, re-entered the kingdom of air, leaving behind the age of water, the most recent of our elemental regressions. That's right, the ages of the Earth express themselves in counterclockwise fashion so we have moved from a time influenced by Pisces, ruled by water and the 12th sign of the zodiac to one influenced by Aquarius, ruled by air and the 11th. It is notable that the quality of the Earth's air during the Aquarian age or paradigm tends to be hot and wet, reflecting the weather phenomena that are already extant. In fact, they are so omnipresent we cannot help but to notice them.

Air corresponds with headiness and you may have already noticed that society in general is becoming more cognizant of thought, as opposed to feelings which were in abundance during the most recent double millennium. Air is also the element where computer science and technology are most at home. And 'A.I.' is a corollary which has only recently become a concern. That the coming years and decades will evidence great change and advancement is a given.

Allora, cosa fareste? (*So what will you do*?) It is my hope that you will continue to recognize societal changes as they occur, embrace the ones you can and work constructively with the ones that you seemingly cannot. The Age of Aquarius is all about 'we' energy, as opposed to the 'me' energy prevalent during the age of Pisces, finding balance between the 'me' and the 'thee.' This requires a re-frame, a re-prioritization of thought and reflexively one's entire manner of thinking. New Age is also about trying something different which I hope most of you are keen on doing.

Benvenuti al nuovo mondo! (*Welcome to the new world*!)

30

FLICKERING

Wondering occurs when the vagaries of electricity are on display, specifically when a lamp or light bulb starts to flicker. Indeed, if something we take for granted suddenly shows itself, reminds us of its presence, it does tend to make us think.

The flicker is a phenomenon that has universal portent. In terms of electricity you may think of it as alternating current, and in truth this is the stuff with which and upon which the Universe functions. The verb form ending in 'ing' is indicative of constancy and continuity for with flickering there is never any question of cessation. Using the terminology of time, flickering occurs during every second of every minute of every day, and in every year, century or millennium.

Generally speaking flickering takes place behind the scenes. You are, therefore, not usually aware of it. However when you are, you are in a moment or moments where it behooves you to really pay attention for that is when miracles often occur.

Another way to think about flickering is to consider one's pulse. You could say it flickers as well. And you could also say it pulsates. The Universe is akin to your heart, a.k.a. the central organ and how it works is to pulsate, to flicker. So in flickering like fireflies what we are doing is maintaining a certain rhythm which applies to the macro, universal principles, as well as the micro, our daily lives. What I am speaking about here is order, the grace from which everything flows.

Candlelight flickers while it is also quite steady. Car batteries flicker internally yet they continue to function for the balance of their shelf life or until their date of expiration. And each human body, too, has a date of expiration but the soul always flickers on. That is the part of our being that has no off switch and it never will.

31

FANS

Of which I had many. And I could have also expressed this thought in present tense because they continue professing their interest. **Donc, c'est un phénomène qui vaut la peine en y penser, au mois un peu** (*therefore it's a phenomenon that's worth thinking about, at least a little.*)

What constitutes a fan and what is their relationship to their "**bien-aimés**" (*those they really like or love.*) You may call yourself a fan when the object of your interest speaks to you energetically. Either you recognize yourself in them or you aspire to be like them. In other words, they are a role model for ways to be in this world. Congruency plays a part, likewise the idea that opposites attract for those that you think of as a shining star may also enable you to see contrast, i.e. how different you and he/she actually are.

Movie stars are often thought of as having a place in the firmament, sports figures as well. In truth you can be a fan of anyone you chose, and they don't necessarily have to be a public figure. Who do you cheer? Who do you feel most comfortable emulating? And who do you never want to be like?

There is also such a concept as 'anti-fan' and I mention this because we are here to love everyone. Bless your negative role models as well and then rest assured in the consciousness of knowing that you are never going to be anything like them. In taking on the role of fan you will be studying all those with whom you are smitten, whatever their rank or the effect you perceive them to have on your persona. Essentially we are speaking of the laws of attraction. Again, like attracts like and opposites attract but they can also repel, possibly even disgust. There is something to be learned from all of your contacts, be they virtual or in the flesh, on screen or just down the block.

A hallmark of any fan is the ability to discern that a certain level of attraction between you and the 'other' exists. Whether or not a relationship ensues and most likely it will not, you remain for some period of time enchanted with those you admire, their **modus operandi** (*ways of being and doing.*)

What did and do fans like about me? I will leave it to them to share those thoughts, when and if they so desire.

32

TRANSITION

The soul is not a fungible commodity; it does not die. It lives, eternally.

Transition is often used as a euphemism for death and in the other languages you know or know of (*speaking to the author and referring to German, Italian, French and Spanish in that order*) if you are **tot**, **scomparso**, **mort** or **fallecido** it is only then that transition occurs, having been triggered by said state of being or condition.

Question: Am I sufficiently prepared for transition?

No, not particularly. As you may already guess the substance of my response, no one is truly prepared for the crossing, the traversing of dimensional boundaries or guidelines. And that is because you cannot prepare and, why is that? Because the experiences you will have as you step outside of your body continue to take shape up until the final breath, including both inhalation and exhalation. You can, of course, speculate (as most of you will) but the actual traversing will be an experience that is uniquely your own, based on/colored by all the thoughts, experiences and knowledge that you may have accrued during your stint in the flesh. My only advice is to be open to it, not to resist when you know that the moment has arrived.

---------------------- *** ----------------------

Ah yes, transition, what we all must joyfully await, well, some of you not so joyfully as the idea of a 'cessation' may not appeal. But, **mes amis**, this is the structure we are dealing with and by we I mean you because this movement, for the time being, is behind me. I would liken death to the flick of a switch, the same kind of switch you use to turn off a light or a given chandelier ~ the cessation, which will be my euphemism for death, the signal that transition is about to occur.

So here is point one; death happens so quickly that time cannot be perceived. And then, once dead, there are a variety of things that could transpire depending on one's personal aperture at the moment of transition. Will you realize that you are suddenly without a physical presence? May-be or may-be not. Will you walk towards the Light? Perhaps not immediately but let me assure you that is what everyone eventually does do. You may be nudged in that direction by a familiar, someone you knew in life or a Spirit Guide. Allow them to do that. Willingness is an important ingredient in this process and resistance is your foe. So, go with the flow...

The Light is where the soul finds itself again, where it truly can be seen. So that is why those who have had near-death experiences speak of having seen a Great White Light. This is so and one of the constants of transition. And when you have moved into that space you will be able, if you want, to explore this new version of self. Actually it is the old version, constantly evolving, but you have not been able to fully see the real you while clothed in a body. The physical self is a lovely thing but as you already know it has a shelf life.

Something else I want to make clear is that any given transition, its ways and means, also the timing of it, are not set in stone. There are no such records in the Akashic sphere. We make these records only as they occur. Therefore much if not everything relating to your transition is not pre-ordained. Every human life-time has quite a bit of flexibility. Some people choose to prolong their physical experiment; other people choose to let go of it at a younger age. All choices are valid and never the twain shall meet. What, say you, is the twain in this case? Definitely not Mark yet you mark your life in such a rich variety of ways. The same is true for passing or, better said, transition.

Again, death is the condition that invites transition: it is the prerequisite, nothing more, nothing less.

33

STATE OF GRACE

You were born into a state of grace and you shall die with that same state intact. Some feel that it is a quality one must work to attain, especially when it becomes clear that the physical body is developing a lack of toleration for the air it breathes, when one's breath becomes labored. These are the final hours, the final minutes and, if within your belief system, a priest or minister may be called or wanted in order to say a few words. The purpose of this, in some minds, is to facilitate a state of grace and I say, "Bless you!" to all who may want this to occur. But I also say "Bless you" to all who do not, those who choose to have a solitary passing or transition. For here, again, is the kernel of truth about this topic: we are born with it and we die with it, whatever may happen or has happened between those two points in time.

Divine Source lives; you know him/her as GOD, the all-encompassing, omnipresent intelligence that finesses the planes of existence. This is a simplistic explanation, I know, but the concept is so vast that even the most enlightened souls have to think twice about how to convey the essence of the everlasting All in All.

Yes, rely on your religious principles (or not) but know that neither stance is a passport to the Other Side; your soul needs no documents to cross this border. Again, you came with grace and you go with grace and this applies to every creature, Earth Plane resident, human or not. In conclusion, being in a state of grace is a constant. It's only your personality that sometimes gets in the way and that's because it's a learning opportunity and if at all disruptive, merely a way station on the road of life.

The fabric of the Universe is clad with grace, yea it is steeped in it.

Again, a state of Grace cannot be earned because you already have it, untethered from personality and reflective of Divine Intelligence.

34

ARS GRATIA ARTIS

(Art for Art's Sake)

While we are on the Earth Plane or shall we say inhabiting it, one of our overall goals is to contribute to its beauty. Beauty, yes, that intangible ~ so we are in the body for many reasons among which is to create something/many things that are beautiful. The most obvious contributor is the artist, perhaps also the architect, but each soul does this in his or her own special way. We could also think about it as contributing to the Greater Good because when you do usually something beautiful is involved: an outcome, an action, a work of art. **Capolavori** sometimes too, what the Italians call masterpieces. But we may add to the quotient that is beauty in myriad ways which have no limits or restrictions.

How you put food on a plate may be beautiful, the sound of your voice, your taste in clothes. The list goes on. I like to call this aspect of human life **ars gratia artis** which translates as art for art's sake. Yes, you can make money at it too, but most who do continually create beauty in all aspects of their lives anyway, not only while they are in the thrall of a cash register.

I once worked for Metro Pictures, the forerunner of MGM. This is MGM's motto and I would agree that said studio has made some artistic pictures. But this phrase is so much more widely applicable. **Soyez des artistes, mes amis**! (*Be artists, my friends*!) Create beauty wherever you go, in whatever you say or do, and you will be building something wonderful. You will be supporting our true motivations, the impulses inherent in the All That Is.

35

SCENT

Rodolfo has requested that I share some of the thoughts he expressed on this topic in "Valentino Speaks" © 2011. Below you will also find a 2023 Addendum.

"Our soul essences are like perfume in the desert. Not only can we smell them clearly, we can sense them from miles away. Nostrils flaring, we are particularly sensitive to our family of origin, able to recognize members of our own soul group by scent alone.

Eau d'âme (*soul cologne*) emits a powerful odor, calling out to those with whom we have the most in common while also announcing our presence to the rest of the world. It's the scent we must live by in order to honor our core selves.

The purpose of having pheromones is to convey information, not only to our own kind but to all species, in each instance producing a specific response. This is how we come to know each other, hopefully promoting greater tolerance for all.

Our sense of smell often takes us beyond ourselves, especially when combined with sight and sound. As Rudolph Valentino, I loved a number of smells, from motor oil to **pasta con vongole** ~ *pasta with clams*, each with a memory attached. Of the five senses, the olfactory was perhaps my favorite. That is why I always liked wearing cologne. In one of my films, scent was crucial to the plot ~ associated with my character's quest for the love of his life as played by Gloria Swanson. Hers was called *Black Narcissus*.

I urge you to adopt a scent of your own as well as experiment with others. There are fragrances to suit every mood. Decide which go well with who you are. Each one you choose must also be compatible with your personal chemistry. What we wear always has the effect of increasing or decreasing our vibratory rates which in turn influences how we are being perceived. Fragrance is no exception. Each scent then, when combined with our own, triggers a specific response.

Fragrances are too often discounted rather than celebrated for what they are. Under no circumstances should we ignore them. Instead, I propose they be thought of as garnishes, wearing them as desired or using them to enhance our environments. In so doing, we would be wise to only pick those that have something to say. Our signature scents, in particular, need to be commensurate with our own brand of being."

Addendum, received in 2023

The olfactory is associated with Taurus, as scent, primarily, is born of the Earth. Of course, fragrances can be distilled in a laboratory and often are but their essences have natural sources so let us not forget that nature, too, can be applied to one's skin or used to create mood in any interior space.

Why not become more attuned to your nose? Why not enjoy scent more than you heretofore have? Ugly smells are like warnings, indicative of things to watch out for, whereas the lovely ones can be likened to gold. Create more gold in your life through the conscious use of fragrance. The silhouette of scent can be a great source of pleasure, enhancing whatever is in progress. Why would the famous **femmes fatales** of the world perfume their boudoirs if this were not so?

A final thought: this is a topic that is sex-less, meaning scent is an equal opportunity employer and/or provider. Not only can one intrigue and be intriguing while wearing scent, one enhances one's own life, adding to the allure of being in the physical body.

36

RVG/WVH CONNECTIONS

RVG and I have many astrological connections, all of which set the stage for the mediumistic work we have been doing for the past twenty years. His birth date, May 6, 1895 at 3PM gives Rudy a Libra rising, ruled by Venus. And his Sun is in Taurus, also ruled by Venus. No wonder he became known as the Latin Lover of the silver screen! Much less is known about his psychic abilities and this is the realm in which he and I connect.

------------------------ *** ------------------------

(*Speaking to the author also, at times, about himself.*)

We shall now continue our literary journey with some introspective comments, the whys and wherefores of how it would come to be that we collaborated on five books thus far with this current one being the sixth. And why have I not addressed this topic before? A matter of timing and now it can be shared, at least in part, as to why this is so.

Obviously you and I have had lots of previous interactions yet it took you a while to wake up to that fact. My films provided the catalyst; they inspired you to consider Rudy and 'his bill of fare.' Also you were intrigued by my having flirted with unseen realms in the company of Natasha and June (*second wife and screenwriter friend*) plus others, of course.

Yes, I have mediumistic abilities as do you, my friend, so you could say 'we put our heads together' and started to write. Your take on the astrological interplay between us is correct but that is only a small portion of what is. Sure, there are karmic reasons which override all and there are liaisons too, primarily of a professional nature that once were ~ where we occupied other bodies in other times and places yet we always knew who was who, always gravitated to each other. And there was also a time of competition that provided stress and an untimely ending. Now we have repaired that rift by doing this work, by co-creating books which have a service component to them, meant to enlighten and instruct, cause to ponder as well.

This is the essence of our connection: **conoscenza** (*acquaintanceship, knowledge*) throughout the eons, also a sense of the simpatico (though with a few hiccups along the way), and so for us this book-writing project has been a glorious time, an opportunity for mutual expansion.

And what about other people with whom I work? Well of course I work with them too, in all forms and manner of forms though differently in each case. For some I am a mentor. With others I am a co-creator as I am with you. Each of these interactions is mutually designed to encourage and nurture our respective enlightenment.

I must communicate. It is my wont to do so and that is why our work occurs, also why I work with other people. All of you have a need to share your skills and wisdom as well so I say it's a mutual admiration society that is totally in sync with who we are, all the beings in question.

And you have met or know of some of them, both virtually and in person.

37

TACITUS

"Truth is confirmed by inspection and delay, falsehood by haste and uncertainty."

So spake Tacitus, one of ancient Rome's most beloved orators and historians. He opined on many subjects, politics and social phenomena among them. And it was his name that spawned an adjective, (*taciturn*) the meaning of which I encourage you to disregard.

One for the ages, Tacitus deserves more scrutiny. I would like to propose him as a role model for he was both astute in his observations and in alignment with the society he was part of, as evidenced by his chronicles of certain events that took place across the reigns of several emperors and their various military campaigns.

Tacitus was not taciturn by the way, a point I've already made. Instead he was a talker and a writer. These are traits I encourage you to adopt. Speak up, speak out, and chronicle your own history especially now when the world is engulfed with half truths or shall we say the 'shadow side.' Return to the facts, as opposed to becoming mired in belief. Sure, have all the beliefs you want but please do not mistake them for facts. There are occasions where belief and fact coincide but that is not commonplace and so the exception rather than the rule. Tacitus worked with facts and from those facts he was able to deduce, creating some beliefs. However, his beliefs, I would say, had factual content, were supported by commonly agreed-upon happenstances meaning that a large number of people had perceived similar things.

Another important aspect of Tacitus' life was his dedication to being a scholar. I suggest you all consider his worth, his import in the march of evolution. We would not know as much as we do without his input. And we will not know as much about 2024 without yours!

I am on a soap box about him, I know, but he was an exemplar – an advocate for consciousness, for astute observation!

38

SALIENT QUOTES

"*We live to live, not to exist.*" ~ *Anon.*

"*Transformation happens when you let it.*" ~ *Sandy Subotnick*

"*Energy, matter, and meaning are three components of reality.*" ~ *Anon.*

"*A timeline is nothing more than a frame of reference, a spine upon which to hang one's experiences.*" ~ *Rodolfo Valentino*

"***L'estasi si fonda sulla bellezza della meraviglia.***" (*Ecstasy is based on the beauty of wonder.*) ~ *Danilo Serra*

"*Viewed from a distance, everything is beautiful.*" ~ *Tacitus*

"*Nothing that's for me will require me to act out of my character to get it.*" ~ *Roberto Di Stefano*

"*History doesn't repeat itself but it often rhymes.*" ~ *Mark Twain*

"*One of our greatest freedoms is how we react to things.*" ~ *Frank Clifford*

"Never think yourself old and you never will be." ~ Janice Horn

"You attract what you are ready for." ~ Roberto Di Stefano

"Most folks are as happy as they make up their minds to be." ~ Abraham Lincoln

"In one sense, we humans are all one: I am you and you are me and they are we and we are all together. But in another sense, each of us is exquisitely special and unique, a miraculous one-of-a-kind character unlike any other ever created in all of eternity." ~ Rob Brezney

*"**Que toda la vida es sueño, y los sueños, sueños son.**" (That all of life is a dream, and dreams, are just dreams.) ~ Pedro Calderón de la Barca*

"Art enables us to find ourselves and lose ourselves at the same time." ~ Thomas Merton

"Man can think of his own life either as the fulfillment of himself, or as the gradual completion of a greater existence of which he is a part and with which he is indissolvably associated." ~ Manly Hall

"When a man also has a friend, God has given him two worlds in which to live." ~ Oscar Wilde

*"**Noi siamo ciò che scopriamo.**" (We are what we discover.) ~ Anon.*

"Every life script is a party to evolution; you did not decide to inhabit a body so that everything about you could stay the same." ~ Rodolfo Valentino

"The only way to deal with an unfree world is to become so absolutely free that your very existence is an act of rebellion." - Albert Camus

"***Disegna la tua vita seguendo le passioni, non le regole***" (*Design your life following your passions, not the rules." - Lorenzo Capuano*

"Kindness is the language which the deaf can hear and the blind can see." - Mark Twain

"***Alcune cose durano un istante ma valgono un'eternità***" (*Some things last an instant but are worth an eternity.) - Anon.*

"We are all one; only egos, beliefs, and fears separate us." - Nikola Tesla

"**Sono molto Valentiniano**." (*I am very Valentinian."*) *- Paolo Orlandelli*

(Something I could also say about myself. Signor Orlandelli, Rome-based actor and director, made this statement in the context of his presentation at the Convegno Valentino, a 2009 symposium on Rudolph Valentino's life and career sponsored by the film department at the University of Turin.)

THURSDAY-FRIDAY
Rudolph Valentino
Wanda Hawley
Pat Moore
Charles Ogle and many other screen celebrities in the splendid picture
The Young Rajah
Rodolph Valentino in the Paramount Picture 'The Young Rajah.'
A Valentino Paramount triumph and comes highly praised.
Pathe News and Good Comedy in Addition
SATURDAY
CONSTANCE TALMADGE in
"THE PRIMITIVE LOVER"
A picture you will enjoy from start to finish, full of the usual good Constance Talmadge twists that make a good Picture
Good Two-Reel Pathe Comedy featuring Will Rogers in "JUST PASSIN' THRU" A Riot
Coming—Doug Fairbanks in "The 3 Musketeers," and "When Knighthood Was In Flower"
The Management of The Liberty Extends to One and All a Merry Christmas

39

THE DUMB SHOW

Or, silent film as an art form. Yes, we were 'dumb' in that we did not speak on celluloid but instead we communicated with our physical selves, especially our eyes ~ a contention made by my former co-star, Gloria Swanson. Indeed, when one stops to think about the visual strength of silent film, it's a wonder to behold. And the plethora of details, subtly expressed, mostly was successful in creating a pleasing and informative whole which was the goal of each production. Directors played a major part in the success of any picture, the script or story line as well, and of course it was up to the actors to convey all of the ideas and emotions of their characters within the world of silence and sparse use of intertitles.

Lieto sono (*I am delighted*) to have worked in this industry making magic with what we had ~ which precluded microphones and, for the most part, the use of color.

We have written elsewhere about each of my films (*in "Rudolph Valentino: The Untold Story"*) but I would like to highlight two of them that for me showed the technical prowess of everyone working behind the scenes. Bravo to those who tweaked the continuity, those who made decisions about the final cuts, those who conceived of the lighting, those who sourced the scenery and props, costume craftspeople and the like! I am grateful for all of your efforts, each of which was designed to enhance the movie-going experience.

I would say "The Eagle" and "Son of the Sheik" are among my best films, and they were made at a time (*1925 and 1926, respectively*) when the artistry of silent film was reaching new heights. Both movies sported certain visuals that were thrilling to audiences, two sequences in particular that involved horses: stopping a runaway carriage which impresses the Czarina in the first, and in the second when I rescue my beloved from the villain at the end of the film. It was also remarkable that I was able to play my character's father (*in "Son of the Sheik"*) via the use of make-up and a split screen. Both films employed camera tricks that had been impossible to accomplish only a few years earlier.

For actors silent films had the advantage of not having to learn lines yet in order to do a good job we had to steep ourselves in our parts, not only to try them on for size but also inhabit them, for we had to fully grasp our character's kinesiology and indeed their id in order to adequately, and sometimes brilliantly, portray them on the screen.

In reality the "dumb show" was not very dumb at all. To the contrary, intelligence reigned for if we were not destined to speak we had to make up for that deficit in other ways, again mostly through the use of our bodies.

40

PANGILIN

In Tagalog: abstinence, avoiding contact with the intent of staying pure.

How and why would I come up with this word? It suits the topic and it is related to Latin as well (***pango*** *is the root word which later morphed to* ***pongo****, used in modern-day Italian and Spanish.*)

So you could also say it's a "ring past not" ~ essentially a line of demarcation. In other words, you are reserving the right to have boundaries, to steel yourself against onslaughts whatever their genesis.

Abstinence is often thought of in a religious sense, the giving up of something, let's say for Lent. I am now suggesting that you apply it far more broadly, in the context of all aspects of your life.

And how do you know when it is time to give something up? How do you know **quando sei stufo**? (*when you have had enough*?)

When you realize that a habit or series of habits have become detrimental to your being, injurious to the healthy function of your chromosomes. There are obvious abstinences, like the need to give up sugar if you are a diabetic and then there are the more subtle ones, like weaning yourself off speculation. The airways are full of speculations, purposely designed to be addictive, to keep audiences in their thrall. In some cases speculation can even veer into the realm of propaganda. So pay attention to what you consume and edit it, at the very least.

You are your own best arbiter of what to abstain from in any and all circumstances. Listen to your heart and head, in that order, and be sure to check in with your nervous system too, as it may also be primed to provide you with a clue.

41

BLAU LICHT

(Blue Light)

Of course White Light is well-known in metaphysical circles, and indeed it is the epitome of manna from Heaven, akin to it, for sure. It's what we invoke when we create circles of protection, what we eventually perceive as we exit the human sphere, what we continuously bathe in while in the **al di là** (*Great Beyond.*) White Light is Life itself. White Light is synonymous with universal energy and symbolic of the Higher Power.

So what about Blue Light? What are its constituencies? Where does it reign? I would say it's a shared phenomenon, part other-worldly and partly Earth-bound. The first thing that comes to mind is the healer, those who practice medicine and all other manner of the healing arts. For you have seen this **Blau Licht** in operation (*speaking to the author*) in the person of a certain Sebastian, he who has the ability to sense the inner workings of every body he encounters in the practice of his profession. This was your most obvious **rendezvous** with Blue Light and its major application, the creation of healing rays.

Sebastian is one of the people who can both conjure it up and also apply it to wherever it's needed in the physical form. He is not, however, unique. There are other people who also know how to direct Blue Light to help heal the human body.

A good way to visualize Blue Light is to think about a gas flame which typically has a blue tinge to it. White Light of course can override Blue Light but in order to heal more quickly and efficiently I propose you see patients surrounded in Blue Light first and then, overall, in the White Light of protection.

Whether they consciously know it or not, artists use Blue Light in furtherance of their creations. Was not Michelangelo, for example, one of these? When an artist creates art in glow of Blue Light, does he not create something breath-taking that also has the power to heal those who behold it? You would not be surprised to learn, therefore, that beauty is ruled by Blue Light or rather that Blue Light is its patron saint.

Blue Light, a force to be reckoned with, to love and cherish as well, for it is one of the phenomena that bridges the dimensions and a symbol of the vitality of the human form.

42

THROUGH A MASK DARKLY

Reviled and feared yet at the same time considered to be a protective device, this, indeed, is the mask.

In the 18th century masks had a frivolous connotation as they were worn to disguise the wearer which would then allow him (or her) to behave in ways other than society's norms would dictate but only within the confines of a specific event such as a party or ball. Venice was an exception to this rule because most of that city's population wore masks during Carnival, a once-a-year event. Venetian masks, however, tended to fully cover the face whereas the 21st century masks most of you are familiar with cover the nose and mouth only, having been constructed with the express purpose of preventing the inhalation of germs.

There is, of course, a debate on the efficacy of today's masks, whether they do indeed protect the wearer as intended.

Completely unrelated to scientific fact, however, is that masks, of late, have become a political football to be tossed around and in many quarters thought of as a sign of repression. What freedoms are being taken away from you by someone else choosing to wear a mask? This I do not know.

On a symbolic level mask-wearing is an equalizer because some of the attributes of each human face cannot be seen when one is masked. So there is a degree of anonymity involved which I would say is the aspect that some people find threatening. The world has been in the thrall of Individualism for centuries, everyone primarily thinking about the Me. Now we are being invited to think more about the groups we frequent or, better said, all those with whom we interact.

With the wearing of a mask, the surgical or medical variety, the impulse is one of protection: to protect yourself from others, specifically potential air-born illnesses, and to protect others should you be harboring germs that for your physical self may be benign while for them they could be toxic.

As an observer the mask to me appears neutral, in other words "no harm, no foul".

43

FRIENDSHIP IN THE 2020'S

Here I am addressing a trend, also speaking from an aspirational point of view.

Friendships are formed for many reasons and sometimes they create strange bedfellows where differences are the attraction rather than similarities. A friendship is based on the magnetism that any two people experience when in each other's presence or sphere of influence. Friendships can also occur virtually as physical proximity is not necessarily a prerequisite for their inception.

Friendship is something we sort of fall into, with neither party being all that conscious of it while in the process of becoming. I would liken it to finding a groove where each individual can be his or her self, relax, and bask in each other's company. And this you may do by finding common ground, shared ideas and ideals, sometimes also goals.

Now I want to add another idea into the mix. There are generational and chronological influences which inject themselves into the free flow of friendship and so this dynamic, like all dynamics, has both fluidity and flavors. The flavor of the 2020's is the resurgence of friendship as a thing, as a goal in and of itself. What I am saying is that there is now a trend to be more cognizant of the friendships you have formed, and are forming, of how they both nurture and further the individuals in question. Interestingly, by the way, some friendships create even stronger bonds than partnerships or marriages.

It is a good idea to evaluate your friendships from time to time, to make sure they continue to be viable. Some last for the fullness of an incarnational cycle; others are far more fleeting. However, all are enriching, learning opportunities in and of themselves. It can be sad to say goodbye to a friend whatever the circumstances but know that good will always ensue, therefore any grief is likely to be brief. And in the great carousel of karma you and your friend may encounter each other again, albeit in other places and spaces.

A final point: agape is what's rampant these days, the love of our fellow human beings ~ a corollary of the Aquarian age. That was the flavor of the 1780's and its resurgence is being duly noted in the present. Therefore this decade is also an era in which great things may be accomplished, for example a reaffirmation of the goals and ideals of the society you inhabit (*making reference to the United States but equally valid for other countries.*)

44

SINGLETON

"A person or thing occurring singly, especially an individual set apart from others."

This, I suppose, is a modern expression but it's perfect for what I want to impart. To wit: that the bottom line of each existence in physical form is to learn the role of singleton and all that entails. We are named upon birth which sets us apart from all others, energetically as well as legally, and we remain an individual while we are interacting with others. For if you do not master your relationship with yourself, how could you possibly "play well with others" ~ behavior your primary school report card once attempted to evaluate (*speaking to the author.*)

As the individual matures, meaning soon after babyhood, learning to love oneself is imperative, learning to nurture oneself too, although many people don't learn how to do either until they are adults and then a few never do, at least not during a given incarnation.

You cannot fully love someone else until you love the singleton that is YOU. This means the personality you are wearing and that of course is the major hurdle. Inside that wrapper we all love our Essence, the core self or soul. That is a given. However the personality can create static and/or encourage one to be overly critical.

Love the singleton, with all of his or her so-called flaws or less desirable elements. Again, they are personality-based, not soul-generated. This will allow you to feel comfortable in your own skin, to fully relax when you are **chez soi** (*at home.*) You need no others to entertain you. It's always nice when they do but you must take on the responsibility of entertaining yourself. And if you become strong in your personhood that is exactly what attracts other people to your energy field. Conversely, if a hole of loneliness is what's being projected who, indeed, wants to fall into that pit? **Alors, aimez-vous bien** (*So, love your selves well!*)

45

ENTERTAINMENT

I come from this world (or rather this is the world I once inhabited), specifically as it had to do with silent film. This is broad subject matter and broad it should be because mostly entertainment, or 'outertainment' because it is sown outside of the singleton paradigm and periphery, is for the purpose of inspiration, thinking about other lives, other scenarios, as a catalyst to propel you towards considering different pathways and/or open your eyes to other possibilities. And cleverness plays a role, too, as this is what engages our attention.

Yes, we live our lives as singletons but we exist in a world of multiplicities.

Entertainment, see it as stimulation, see it as the zest for life it often is. Being entertained co-exists with one's solitary self, quite nicely actually, so it's what I would call a symbiotic relationship. And that is why I have chosen to deal with this topic sequentially, immediately following our most recent discussion.

You, the human entity, spend a lot of time looking inward and that is as it should be. Entertainment allows one to get outside of oneself once in a while, to be carried away while being inspired. What better combination than that?

The planet Neptune rules the entertainment industry because it is reflective of the world of dreams, glistening generalities delivered with charm and precision, often in capsule-like form so that they may be easily understood.

This book is also a form of entertainment because it exists outside of the self.

46

INTRAMONTABILE

(*Timeless*)

We think a lot about time, the passage of it, the effect of it, the impact of it. What about its opposite, **intramontabile**, where time is irrelevant or does not matter?

The soul is not, strictly speaking, subject to time; therefore. timeless because it exists in all times and places, some would say simultaneously although we can only perceive one particular time as it relates to the overall trajectory of a given life cycle. We also know that soul energy cannot be torn asunder. It is therefore **intramontabile**, not subject to the vagaries associated with human understandings. Neither is universal energy in the form of White Light subject to any time constraints. It simply IS.

That said, pay less attention to your watches, **mes amis**, or the clocks you see, or the additional candle on the birthday cake. Think, rather, about what is timeless. I challenge you to find any number of things that easily fit into this category.

It is also really helpful to think about yourself as timeless because you are. The physical body has limits placed on its viability and indeed it is quite a complex mechanism, full of correspondences that the soul who is animating it may take for granted. Though it's often been said that you outlive your body, please allow me to repeat that fact ~ one more time!

The you that is YOU is your essence; your physicality is what enables it to play dress-up.

47

BONDINGS

The human species has a tendency to bond, in innumerable ways. Some bondings are quite temporal such as when a random group of people suddenly find themselves in the same work environment, office or corporation. True you may end up working with each other for years and it's also likely that you will not. Twenty-first century workplaces tend to churn their employees a fair amount.

The concept of bonding, primarily, has to do with those with whom we identify: the residents of our own city, state, country (also our professional colleagues and family members) plus, of course, our ancestry or mix thereof. A bonding requires the willingness of at least two people to see themselves as part of the same group but usually they are comprised of larger numbers. There are also geographical subsets. In the United States, for example, most Californians are quite aware of the uniqueness of the entire West Coast. And as a southern Italian, I bonded with others over the natural beauty that was rampant in early twentieth century

Los Angeles and very much reminiscent of my homeland in look and climate. I also bonded with my compatriots in the film industry.

One may even bond over trifles, such as liking the same colors or brands of cars.

The larger metaphysical question here is: what brings singletons together? The short answer is possibility and a desire to become associated with others of like mind and/or experiences. There is also the issue of strength in numbers, of validation, of pride. Watch any parade and you will note that they are made up of many different kinds of bondings, a.k.a. reasons for being. Sure, we can fully BE as a singleton but we can also BE more within or as a part of a bonding. Although you don't actually need to bond with anyone or any group per se, and that's because you came in with everything you need in order to be successful on your own, bonding with others will enrich your experiences greatly.

48

ARTIFICIAL INTELLIGENCE

Can intelligence ever truly be artificial? Is it not organic by nature?

What we may think of as artificial springs forth from the mind of a creator, the flesh and bone kind, for a program must be created by someone in order for it to take hold. Therefore so-called artificial intelligence has human roots and, reflexively, divine permission. Nothing exists in a vacuum; every thing has correspondence.

Again, it's an illusion that A.I. functions completely on its own. It only seems to self-generate once a particular program or piece of software has been turned loose or brought online. What is going to challenge us now is how artificial intelligence is ultimately put to use. Nefarious types may employ it to further blur the line between truth and conjecture, literally putting words in other people's mouths for their own purposes. So it could become a tool for propaganda OR an overall aid to mankind.

We have trepidation for what we don't know or are as yet unaccustomed to. A.I. is just another thing requiring that the art of discernment be applied. The media, as we write, seems to be fanning the flames of hysteria because A.I. has suddenly been deemed newsworthy. True, like many other things in the hands of the wrong people it could be dangerous but it is also capable of producing marvelous results, and we don't yet know the extent to which it could or should function. So trial and error, at least for the present, will continue to be the rule of the day.

Some might go so far as to say that artificial intelligence is satanic. Not so, **mes amis**, in and of itself. Yet the 'Svengali' who controls it might be, or become, thoroughly warped. This is the danger that is likely to test us, governments and individuals alike, as we continue becoming acquainted with the Aquarian age.

The book is still being written about A.I. Therefore, I cannot say what shape it will actually take once fully formed. Cautions are advised, however. Fiction versus fact, hasn't that always been the work of individual discernment? As 'body-wearers' you have lots of decisions to make and this technology presents us with a whole new slew of potential arrows.

49

EXHAUSTION

Physical & Spiritual

Exhaustion is, of late, a major theme with all of you 'earth-bounders.' It is, unfortunately, part and parcel of the momentous changes currently afoot and, if you don't get tired of business as usual, what could or would possibly inspire you to make changes? And then we must also split this topic into two parts.

The physical side is easy to recognize and that carries over into the mental realm because your faculties are housed in your physical vehicle. Sometimes it's difficult to distinguish which is which, the rhetorical question: Am I just physically tired, worn out by repetition and the abhorrent behavior so rampant in today's society or, have I been working too hard, pushing my body too much or, am I not able to take in another fact and/or would-be or pretend fact? All of this is a recipe for overloaded circuits and highly understandable. And over-dosing energetically is quite common these days plus, strangely enough, necessary for the general evolution of mankind.

What I must take issue with is the idea of spiritual exhaustion, for the spirit itself may never become **épuisé** (*worn out.*) There is always more where spirit is concerned, more to give and more to receive. Spirit is **débordé**, meaning the cup runneth over. There are no limitations where spirit is concerned. And it is this fact that will see you through any disturbance in "the force," so to speak, or, better said, the status quo.

50

NIHILISM

We are preparing for major changes at every level of society. Those who are nihilistic or behave nihilistically are catalysts for change. When a system has been set in stone it calls attention to itself, saying "Change Me! Change me!" And there are people, individuals who, having been born within a given framework of time, will gleefully fulfill this role, tear down what is so that what isn't yet may take hold and therefore grow.

This work seems to have grave implications. And in truth it does. Yet society can never change without the presence of at least a few active nihilists. Nihilism is a precursor to a whole new way of living which involves being far more heart-centered than the great majority of current Earth inhabitants.

So it's a general and gradual change I speak of here, not a revolution or full reign of chaos, but definitely there's going to be some degree of 'mixing it up' ~ no doubt about that!

51

EVOLUTIONARY DRIVERS

"Picture your life as the face of a clock. At certain points of the entablature evolutionary drivers come into play, moments in time that shock us out of our complacency and stupor." - Glen Perry, Astrologer

Mr. Perry also suggests, and rightfully so, that we cooperate with the "evolutionary imperative at the heart of the Cosmos" which is to say that we always do our best to be in sync with what we, ourselves, have proposed in terms of evolutionary goals. Things do not haphazardly just happen; they are part and parcel of each individual life script and can only to be triggered when the time is right. Sometimes the catalyst may be an astrological tick, a movement of the minute hand on your personal clock prompted by a specific alignment, or misalignment, of a planet or planets. At other times it's an event or another person that causes us to veer from our "rut," which means whatever we may view as standard practice.

Yes, there could be many contributing factors when one is on the precipice of change but the best analogy is that you drive your own car. Therefore, you are always in charge of your own evolution. Situations or people may nudge you in one direction or another but you can choose to ignore them, also choose to initiate evolutionary change on your own, unrelated to outside factors.

That said, it is a given that every life script is a party to evolution. You did not decide to inhabit a body so that everything about you could stay the same.

Whether macro or micro, evolutionary drivers are always in place and in the throes of functioning. Indeed, they never take a break. When societies change, those who inhabit them change as well. This we can chalk up to evolution because nothing is ever at rest. Nothing remains constant even when it appears that it does. Something is always in the process of evolving. And we came into the body to do, let's say, more 'tangible' evolving, at least that is how most of us perceive it. Of course you could also make the case that nothing on the Earth Plane is all that tangible but we are not here to talk about physics or the essence of matter.

What's important to understand is that a 'driver' could have many manifestations, could be just about anything or anyone. We have people in our lives that provide fodder for evolution, opportunities for growth. And we also experience things that have a similar cause and effect. "Ain't it grand?," as one of my contemporaries once said (*referring to Mae West.*)

Evolutionary drivers may come at us from any and all angles. Pay attention, therefore, to which way the wind is blowing.

52

TRADITION

(*Continuing pattern of beliefs and practices; a customary method or manner.*)

There are a myriad of definitions for this term yet these are the aspects of it that I would like to call to your attention.

When does tradition serve you and when does it not?

Voi, americani, particolarmente, (*You, Americans, especially*) this is what seems to be up, what has risen, like cream, to the top of a bottle of unpasteurized milk.

Tradition is usually entwined with history, or at least the perceptions of such. History, one could say, does carry it forward often in an unbroken line in the form of impulses.

And impulses or energy waves emitted in a given country have their own flavors and this is often conveyed in said country's traditions.

Having lived in the United States during the adult portion of my life, I shall endeavor to tailor my remarks to the present political and cultural situations.

It's getting more obvious by the day that some of the mores of this land need to be tweaked or significantly changed. Many of the rules that your Congress abides by, for example, are based on tradition, not law, and there comes a time for more codification, more clearly defined 'rules of the road.' That time is now, or was yesterday. We are dawdling as a country and all because some people think there is nothing that should or could be changed. Too much of a "that's the way things are; live with it" kind of attitude.

And then there are aspects of this country's traditions, socially-speaking, that need revitalization and sprucing up ~ **e pluribus unum**. This is a multi-cultural land, by definition, yet it continues to be torn asunder by 'othering' ~ subsets of the population seen as unworthy or undesirable, economically, ethnically, racially, whereas in truth that is just not so for the human condition is fully present in each and every one of us.

By law all those residing in the United States have certain rights. And here I do not distinguish between citizens and non-citizens; I speak of human rights, all human rights.

Traditions must hold harmless all those within their thrall. Therefore they should be examined from time to time. And if any are found deleterious, they need to be purged or at the very least in some way realigned. There are negative American traditions like a penchant for racism and positive ones such as adherence to the principals of the constitution ~ if not to every word or thought it contains.

"Accentuate the positive, eliminate the negative, and don't mess with Mister In-Between."

("Ac-Cent-Tchu-Ate the Positive" ~ popular song from 1944, music by Harold Arlen and lyrics by Johnny Mercer.)

53

CELL PHONE ADDICTION

Do you not want to look up from your phone? Is the artificial screen more important to you than the one presented to us by nature? Are you breathlessly awaiting the next text or tweet?

Depending on how you answer these questions you may indeed have become hooked.

This is a phenomenon of your time and something to be cognizant of so that you can choose, from moment to moment, how you truly want to spend your time. Sure, the cell phone is a business requirement in many instances but it does not have to be a personal necessity to the extent it often is ~ unless you say so.

There is nothing that can take the place of personal experience, and certainly not the virtual world. You may use virtual means for intellectual comprehension but not to procure emotional depth. Only real-life situations can provide that. And by real-life, I mean interactions with other people and/or entities.

The toy, the appendage, the symbol of communication and interconnectivity, these are some of the most notable aspects of a cell phone, part and parcel of its **raison d'être**.

Remember, as a child, when you had a favorite toy? As an adult that might be your cell phone. And for some people having a cell phone could be even more important than having a functioning arm or hand, hence my comparing it to an appendage. Then there's the issue of communication and the impulse to be connected which has become an imperative, a function of our suddenly being hurtled into the Aquarian age where being connected is a major goal, in and of itself.

So cell phone psychology has lots of elements to it and the author of this book knows wherefore I speak. To wit: cell phone use must be balanced and it is not the be-all and end-all of 21st century existence. In other words, don't get carried away and don't solely conduct your life on the screen of a cell phone. Instead, continue to embrace at least a few other alternatives and you will be better off for having done so.

54

M.A.G.A.

In recent years the use of this acronym has become required in certain circles, repeated daily in some cases - perhaps more often than not. It has entered the lexicon and implanted itself into mass consciousness.

Let me now address my own viewpoints and reactions.

'Make America Great Again.' When, my friends, has America not been great? It was great before I got there and it was great in 1913 when I landed at Ellis Island. It was great when I first went to Hollywood and especially great towards the end of my life when my career peaked, and it has been great since, in large and small ways.

I particularly have a problem with the 'again' portion of this acronym for it implies greatness has waned, or did wane, at some point in time. When was that, **mes amis**? I am wondering if anyone could or would tell me. The implication of this appellation is all about ethnicity - some magical moment in the history of the United States when it was not a melting pot, when there were no immigrants. That time never was, and never will be. This phrase also implies the existence of 'pure blood' Americans, whatever that might entail. We are all bastards, I must say, with antecedents that vary greatly, and 'greatly great' is what made us who we are. Indeed, we are already great, no making required, and so certainly the 'again' portion of this slogan is a misnomer and absolutely incomprehensible.

Did people ever look askew at me? Of course they did, and Italians, especially southern Italians, were not welcome in every corner. Yet I relied upon my upbringing, good manners, and a sense of style to bridge the gap and indeed I was successful. America gave me the space to be who I really was and I achieved heights there that would have been unattainable in Europe during those very same years. For me America is great and will always be. Will it, as a country, have self doubts? Will there be political chaos from time to time? Will the economy gyrate once in a while? Of course the answer is Yes to all of these questions. However these are growing pains, refinements of sorts that continue to refresh the essence of this great experiment that is democracy, American style. As an outsider I became an insider. I can see 'what is what' ~ both then and now. Do not allow democracy to slip from your fingers; hold on tight, even if it's a bumpy ride.

Courage, mes amis! Restez forts! (*Be brave, my friends; stay strong!*)

55

1942

(Speaking to the author and making reference to his birth year to facilitate this discussion.)

Nineteen forty-two marked the beginning of your current incarnation. It was a shadowy period in history when extremes reigned and wars were being waged, not a peaceful time to be born. And you have surfed some rough waves in the intervening years as well as crested, many, many times. These ups and downs are indicative of a full life as symbolized by a heart-beat. No one 'straight-lines' themselves through an incarnation; there is always also contrast.

These present moments are some of the most unstable since your birth. But, my friend, you carry it all well; you pace yourself on what you inhale or consume in terms of the airways and what they contain; all of this is good.

Cycles tend to repeat themselves and now again we have flirtations with fascism or the outright adoption of such. This is my warning to you, dear readers: by whatever names, fascism, authoritarianism, oligarchy, these are detrimental to the true spirit of mankind and incompatible with the Aquarian Age, like putting a stick in a wheel or attempting to do so. The dictators of the past, in some cases, seem like they've reincarnated. Just how concerning is that? To answer my own question, "Very!"

56

A HOUSE IS NOT A HOME

You (*speaking to the author*) have visited a number of the great palaces of Europe, most recently the **Regia di Caserta** of the Kingdom of the Two Sicilies. You have also been to **Versailles** in France, **Schönbrunn** in Austria, and the royal palace in Turin as well as many of the mansions in Newport, Rhode Island. Hard to call any of these extravaganzas "homes" yet that is what they purported to be - exquisite and sumptuous perhaps but in some cases also quite stilted and stuffy.

What defines a home as opposed to a house? Primarily it is intimacy, my friends. Can intimacy thrive there and how does one go about creating the space for it to occur?

It is often in the context of love that homes are established. Natacha and I had such fun playing around with our environment in her Sunset Boulevard bungalow and that continued when we moved to Whitley Heights (*both properties were in Hollywood.*)

A house is a physical structure which serves as an anchor in the material world. It is where you conduct your life and the place from which you locomote. It is also where you lay your head and a marker of sorts, just like your name. People can often find you there if they look. A house does not necessarily a home make. Neither does an apartment or any other kind of living arrangement.

How to define home? It's where you feel comfortable, where you can express your tastes, where you can be intimate, where you can truly let go and utter a sigh of relief. It's also a place to entertain family and friends, to give and receive.

Perhaps you will now see where you live in a different light. Home spaces are sacred; the Romans honored that concept by creating altars in their houses which in some cases included maintaining an eternal flame.

(*Speaking to the author*) I noticed a vision of Pompeii dancing through your mind while we were writing the previous sentence!

"*What is it about a house that makes it seem so familiar*?" - *Edith Wharton*

57

PUNTER

(*Colloquialism with several meanings: Ordinary Joe; someone who hopes to make a quick profit via improbable or risky bets; opportunist, also known as a chancer.*)

This is a frame of reference primarily used in the UK and it is also quite applicable to certain people who live in the United States. In fact, it's both a feature and a fixture. Americans, in particular, are big on trying their luck which of course is fine when there are no adverse implications. However, if rolling the dice involves putting something over on someone else - "Ah, there's the rub!" Schemers and reivers need not apply. Unfortunately trickster-ism has become widely accepted and to some extent is baked into the system.

Though perhaps not expressly stated, Wall Street does believe that 'greed is good' and the to and fro of the market is reflective of the constant churn of financial instruments. There is also the issue of Americans wanting to be seduced by what they consider to be a bargain or good buy. As a result, discount opportunities proliferate and the sucking sounds you hear are tentacles being surreptitiously attached to your bank accounts. How many providers, for example, want you to arrange for automatic payments which later you discover are almost impossible to cancel?

Yes, the Earth Plane operates on the principle of money and goods being exchanged. What I am saying is to simply be more cognizant of your "wants" as opposed to outside sources trying to instill needs that are not relevant to your inner self or essence. Spend your money wisely; spend it foolishly too, if you want, but don't allow yourselves to become unduly influenced or manipulated, either by particular individuals or the media in general.

Punters are often also hucksters. I believe that is an American term for aggressive businesspeople or politicians. A huckster is not necessarily 'running a game' yet they could be. **Méfiez-vous** (*watch out*) or at the very least be a bit cautious.

In succeeding years some aspects of American consumerism are bound to grind to a halt. More consciousness shall be devoted to quality as opposed to quantity, to practicality as opposed to **bagatelles** (*trifles*) ~ all of which indicate a major change of perspectives. Though I have harped on this before, these shifts may be chalked up to the beginning of the Aquarian age which has a "Three Musketeers" flavor: "one for all and all for one."

58

PSYCHIC ABILITIES

Everyone has them, including you! However, will you choose to activate them or will they remain fallow? That is the question.

I liken the potential use of these abilities to exercise, of which I was a big fan. I even wrote a short book on that topic back in the day. First you need a catalyst to awaken them and then exercise in order to bring them to fruition as well as hone your capacity to competently and carefully work with these gifts. For psychic abilities are indeed gifts and not to be perverted, trifled with, or in any way mismanaged!

The word psychic only means that some segment of your consciousness is either in contact with or can contact other realms, potentialities, or timelines - sometimes off-planet entities as well.

What a psychic typically imparts are probabilities, hunches and perceptive introspections, also messages from your spirit guides. And if this information can be helpful to those on the receiving end, so much the better! A psychic can never tell you what to do and neither should anyone ever attempt to use their psychic abilities in this manner.

Each and every decision we make is, in the final analysis, self-generated and reflective of the soul making it. If we allow someone else's will or subliminal suggestions to get in the way, we will just have ourselves to blame.

It may be interesting to note that I developed my psychic muscles during my most recent earthly sojourn, especially in the company of Natacha (*Rudy's second wife*) and June Mathis (*his screenwriter friend and mentor.*) Then we were automatic writers, receiving information from the spirit world and our respective guides in this fashion. Wayne, (*referring to the author*) had also been working on this aspect of self prior to our coming together to co-create books. His first channeling experience was with his friend Janice, not long after she entered the Astral (*"Letters from Janice" © 1987.*) Therefore he was already an adept, though perhaps slightly rusty, when we started to work on "Valentino Speaks" (© *2011.*) And our meeting of the minds continues, to this very moment and beyond!

One does not need to be an automatic writer to exercise one's skills as a psychic. Neither does one need to be a voice medium. However, if you are presenting yourself to the world as a psychic you may want to use a tool, cards for example, or an object with which you can connect to the moment and/or the person in question. And if your psychic abilities are being expressed spontaneously, go with the flow and share only what can or might empower those 'to whom it may concern.' Plus, always cast pearls, never pellets.

59

BODY BUGS

Genetic Rendezvousing/Appointment with a Gene

Not the creepy crawly kind, but rather what may be inherent in the machinery. Did you not know that your physical self has a perpetual element to it so that once set in motion at birth it blossoms forth and continues to operate forthwith, for all practical purposes on automatic pilot? For example, no one has to specifically think about lifting a leg or opening their mouth for it to happen. All bodily functions are much more subtle than that, based on muscle memory and will power.

Here we talk about genetic code for indeed we have all been coded, coded ourselves, and inherent in that are usually predispositions and predilections. And while we swim in our respective gene pools, certain things will eventually become apparent such as where the bugs are, which glitches are likely to appear and/or make manifest over time. You may even find specific body parts being deemed by doctors as problematic and therefore according to them doomed to experience some sort of **faiblesse** or weakness.

If you will, allow me to turn a noun into a verb where heretofore there never was one, I propose "re-quarking" as a solution. When born we are "pre-quarked" meaning that every particle of every gene, cell or atom has been individually chosen and then integrated into the whole. By countermanding the quarks as needed or required, re-adjusting them to some extent, you can achieve better function and more optimal outcomes.

How does one know when to undertake such a project? When evidence suggests some sort of **discesa** or downhill movement in body function I urge you to visualize your genetic material in a different, more perfect light. See it whole and it will be or at the very least you will be putting the brakes on what might become a trend. For trends there are and ever more shall be, having been set into motion by genetic rendezvousing, the intersection of predispositions on a particular genetic pathway or timeline. Go instead for how you would prefer things to be, by consciously turning your thoughts in that direction. **Luce, luce, luce, dovunque**! (*Light, light, light, everywhere*!) Miracles happen, all the time!

The power is always in your hands, **mes amis**. All that is required is intention. You alone decide the length of your incarnation; you also have a say in body function and you can alter any course of genetically-based eventualities by re-framing and re-organizing your individual quarks.

60

LINEAGE

Lignaggio/Lignée/Estirpe

From whence you came, your ancestors and gene pool. I have chosen to write about this because it directly relates to what preceded it, our most recent topic.

We inherit both strengths and limitations from our ancestors. We are proud of them; we are aware of their ethnicities, their struggles and triumphs. And we usually know something about their history, especially true today given the expansion of knowledge, also search engine viability.

I was always proud of my **lignaggio** and I was as proud of the French aspects of my being as the Italian which, because I was born in Italy, tended to predominate. I was delighted to find out that my maternal grandfather, Pierre Barbin, had been an engineer, designing bridges that were vital to the expansion of the Italian railroad system. In fact, one of his achievements was near the city of my birth, spanning a ravine. On my father's side of the family, I was thrilled that there had been some self-styled aristocrats, the **di Valentinas**, who became the inspiration for my name change after I moved to Los Angeles. And he was no slouch himself, my father, having been schooled in Veterinary arts which gave him an intimate knowledge of all things having to do with nature. My mother also had a keen mind and was well-educated, primarily in France. She and I often saw eye to eye in discussions. I inherited some of my parents' talents, some of their limitations as well, especially in relation to quarks or gene composition.

Now we shall talk about you as an example (*speaking to the author*) and then draw some conclusions. I could go into your roots, how you also have western European antecedents, varied nationalities or ethnic groups in your background, how some of your ancestors came early to the United States prior to its inception while others came later, mostly during the 19th century. All this is interesting and similar things are also true for others, no matter which country of the world they now inhabit.

Family lore provides you with strength but it is also at the present time limiting your possibilities. You have bought into the idea, for example, that everyone in your blood line dies within a certain age range. This is erroneous thinking. Remember, every incarnation is elastic, has a stretchable component to it, and therefore you are not constrained by anything your ancestors did or did not do. That also applies to length of life or the elongation of an incarnation.

As we write you are working on this, going inward, developing mantras that countermand the guff doctors propose, their contention that a given age is likely to be evidenced by certain manifestations in the form of ailments or cautionary tales, some of which could possibly prove to be fatal. Bah, I say, humbug. Time to change horses and/or streams, pursue different avenues of probability!

61

MEDIA

The Proliferation of Punditry

I was once a member of the media and still am. I speak indirectly now, of course, yet also very directly as is my wont. You all know me as Rodolfo, once upon a time star of the silver screen. It is through Wayne and other channels that I now share information and ideas ~ not by appearing in films or writing my own books as these are some of the things I can no longer do given my current status as a non body-wearer.

The media has always been a powerful creature. And it continues to morph, constantly shape-shifting. Now you live in the digital age whereas in my day it was the written word that prevailed. Like any actor I longed for good reviews in the newspapers of note and sometimes I got them, especially for roles like Julio in "The Four Horsemen of the Apocalypse." A particularly favorable aspect of my film career was that many of my movies were based on books, in some cases quite famous ones. I was also fortunate to have June Mathis in my corner as screenwriter and friend. She liked to incorporate metaphysical concepts into her scripts and I am thinking of "The Young Rajah" when I say that. Though panned at the time, the ideas it contains still shine forth.

I never fully learned to manage the media although it definitely played a big part in making me a star and for that I'm eternally grateful. But at the same time I was aware that what I did, on screen and in my personal life, might be subject to emulation or derision and those were the phenomena that came to pass, during my lifetime and after.

The media is like a leviathan that can easily swallow you whole. If you are somehow 'in the media' ~ either a member of it or being reported on, make sure to keep swimming faster than it does!

Also the media has always had a slant to it, even in the messages of yesteryear chiseled in stone or typeset prior to being printed. Now it is the '**sprechen**' that rules, what people say, specifically those who identify themselves as pundits as well as those who claim to be commenting on the news when in reality they are merely speculating.

It is only through editing your intake, your own consumption of media, that you may discern the real nuggets or crux of the matter at hand. And you really ought to consider a variety of sources whereas if you continually return to the well of singular focus, one primary font of information, you are apt to be fooled and likely more often than not.

You, too, may find yourself in the role of a pundit one day. All well and good, I say; just make sure to know wherefore you speak, and that your opinions are measured and just.

62

INTERNET

When was the last time you read about the internet in this type of book? Probably never!

The name of the thing is very graphic. It implies webbing and indeed the internet is also known as the web. Webs may also be perceived as intriguing as oft they are. The internet was born for a reason. It's time had come around 1995. The hints of a new world were already afoot then and what better instrument for those phenomena to be able to develop than this one? The internet cannot be seen; neither can the bond that exists among all living creatures, mankind and the other species. Yet we need tangibility to bond, to fully become aware of the other.

With an internet connection everyone is only one keyboard away; international friendships flourish and business is also integral to this new-ish paradigm. The internet promotes connectivity, specificity, and a larger viewpoint as well. Without it we would not be able to fully grasp the Aquarian Age, the age of relating, of consideration for the other, and the enlightenment that is to come ~ in these years and those that follow. The internet is your tool, an example of what can be and is. It provides us with a window on the world and a lens with which to view it, equally important.

Some things are meant to be. Such is the concept of the internet as well as its implementation which at the present time is still under development. "Men and Women Working" would read the sign were there to be one. This is the phenomenon that is helping society adapt as it simultaneously offers challenges and opportunities for growth.

63

ACCESO

(*Turned On*)

As sparks of Divinity we are always turned on, at least in principle. When in the body, however, we may allow our spark to be dimmed or in some cases almost extinguished. This is not a helpful choice, neither is it desirable. The fact is having a body between your inner self and the outer environment, as you see and feel it, requires more push, more heft. That's why remaining turned on is even a topic.

You must, while wearing a body, shine ever brighter. And how, **mes amis**, does Rudy propose that this may be accomplished? Conscious aiming, I say, is the proper response, projection. Make it be known that you are interested and you will automatically become interesting - to yourself and others. 'Shine on Harvest Moon' - an old adage perhaps but it can't hurt. Every day search out pieces of reality that attract you. Whether or not they are random is irrelevant; it's simply your interest and the levels thereof which keep you turned on, make you a viable human being, especially during this particular tranche of the 21st century.

Restez branchés, autant que possible (*Remain plugged in, as much as possible*) and you will have rendered a great service to all mankind!

64

GOD

Exquisite Chronology

He/She eternally merits upper case. Throughout the eons mankind has always felt the presence of a Greater Intelligence, the existence of a master plan. In attempting to explain it, lots of personalization occurred in the form of lower case gods epitomizing both virtue and vice ~ Venus, for example, as opposed to Mars ~ or if you will, the atom that is GOD split into various micro-particles, each one purporting to explain and support a particular sphere of influence or celestial operation.

Divine Intelligence reigns; this term of course is a synonym for GOD. Think about any and all good works that human beings may ever do for one another and you will have only an approximate summation of the Love that is expressed of GOD. Such Love is as all-encompassing as you have heard: omniscient, omnipresent, omnipotent. There is no 'not GOD.' Nothing can override Love and Love is GOD. GOD is also the animating principle and the Sun is one of the best examples of it, accessible to all mankind.

So why do I associate chronology with GOD, the march of time? Because it is a facet of the All That Is and therefore one of His/Her expressions, perhaps what is most likely to grab your attention, and at many different points in the earth-bound sojourns of any life cycle.

GOD: the Wonder of wonders, also called the King of kings. There are not enough superlatives in any language to describe the vastness of the All in All which of course is yet another synonym for GOD. The keeper of the mountains, the lord of the seas, everything that is of Earth is also of GOD. The lands I inhabit, if we could call them that, are likewise ruled by Consciousness, the largest most all-encompassing one there ever was or ever could be. I can only tiptoe around the concept that is GOD as there is no way to adequately describe this phenomenon and yet I shall give it a try. Consciousness above all other consciousnesses: this is perhaps as close as I can get to a more precise definition.

When do human beings tend to think most about GOD? When they are born and/or die, when they marry as well – if they do, when their children are born and they witness the miracle of life, but not necessarily in the service of organized religion. Might I be a Deist as were many of the thinkers during the Age of Reason? **Peut-être que oui, mes chers amis** (*perhaps that is so, my dear friends.*)

I once embraced a singular religion. Now I know GOD is all religions in all times and places so one religion is never more desirable than any other. GOD loves all; GOD is All.

65

SUN

Our constant companion and perhaps the most obvious example of the animating principle, this is the star around which we revolve as we strive to evolve, our reason for 'being' on the Earth Plane. The Sun is GOD ~ in action. So are the other stars you see in the sky and the planets that whirl around them.

Raw energy is always visible on a clear day. That is when we can see the Sun, our most obvious generator ~ our most apt model of life enhancement. For we cannot be fully healthy without coming into contact with the rays of the Sun because human beings also absorb its energy as does every other living thing that walks the Earth or rests there upon, animal, mineral, vegetable.

Il Sole ci da anima (*the Sun makes us feel alive.*) It is soul-nourishing and symbolically a sign of happiness. People often equate a sunny day with feeling upbeat. Indeed, the Sun (feeling it/seeing it) makes us happy. One could also say that it's a constant reminder of the presence of GOD.

The Sun is a stand-in for the concept of Light as it's Light in physical form. It teaches us how all-encompassing, all-enveloping Light is - by its very existence, by the sense that it is eternal for to us it seems so. You may also conceive of the Sun as a consistent combustion machine which it most definitely is. Only at night does the Sun seemingly take a rest while shining elsewhere on Earth instead.

Gott im Himmel, Das ist die Sonne und wir sind ihre Kinder/leben im Kindergarten. (*GOD in Heaven, this is the Sun and we are its children/live in the kindergarten.*)

66

DISCIPLINE/SACRIFICE/SUFFE RING

These three are a triumvirate; they are indeed linked even if it may not seem so at first glance. Discipline, as well as sacrifice and suffering, are only beneficial if in operation for or on behalf of the Greater Good - Greater Good for yourself and for others or for the society in which you live. Sometimes they operate singularly as well because discipline does not necessarily lead to suffering, etc. We discipline ourselves to help ourselves, also to be sensitive to the needs of others. We do not suffer for ourselves for if we do I would call it a case of great selfishness. We may sacrifice ourselves in certain situations but, I would caution, never to one's own detriment with no greater motive involved. Doing so would be akin to self-flagellation.

Trying to save someone else's life is a demonstration of all three: discipline to know what to do, sacrifice by rolling the dice, and suffer some perhaps as a result of your good deed. But know, **mes amis**, that all good deeds are magnified many fold on the wheel of karma so you, too, shall reap the rewards ~ if not immediately then eventually.

67

ALEXANDER THE GREAT

In every era there are people who stand out ~ for their deeds, their perspicacity, their forbearance, and their often uncanny perceptions. Alexander is one of those, he who almost single-handedly covered the Mediterranean Sea and some of the lands beyond it with the Hellenistic veil. He was the conqueror, invader, also bringer of Light, for there were many aspects of Greek society that were quite enlightened, especially as they pertained to scholarly pursuits and the realm of philosophical introspection. Indeed, Alexander is a study in luminosity. So shimmering was he that he drew others to him like moths to a flame. Though not necessarily always a good thing, this phenomenon was an important aspect of his dynamics and one of the reasons people clamored to be in his company, militarily and otherwise.

Like mine his life was short and also like mine it was complete and well-lived. I am not comparing myself to Alexander, **non, mes amis**, for I did not possess his abilities with a sword nor some of his other attributes. I would say, however, that we both inspired people, though for very different reasons.

From a metaphysical point of view Alexander was able to quicken time, also stretch it out, and I say this because his impact was so far-reaching and long-lasting. Following his death, his compatriots carried on, spreading Greek influence throughout the ancient world. One of his generals came to sit upon the throne of Egypt in Alexandria, its library eventually becoming celebrated as one of the greatest of all time. Ptolomy established a dynasty, the last one, starting with himself and ending with his descendant, Cleopatra. The net result was that Greeks ruled Egypt for 275 years before the Romans added it to their empire.

The reason I chose to salute Alexander here is because genius walks among ye, in 2023. As this decade continues to unfold, look for those who likewise shimmer, those whose luminosity attracts. Not all of them will be perfect but their job is not to achieve perfection but rather to be way-showers or exemplars. The Earth Plane needs some new heroes and most assuredly they shall be supplied.

68

LE CHIAVI

(*Keys*)

Not the kind on a chain or those hanging from the skirt of a **châtelaine** (*keeper of the keys in a French château.*) The ones I am talking about are clues and they are likely to be found everywhere. If you will, picture an empty field, flat land with no vegetation, not even a weed. Yet there is a noticeable indentation in the landscape, therefore a clue that may be worthy of investigation. Could it indicate the presence of water, be where an animal lives, or is it evidence of danger, the man-made kind?

So here is point one: when a clue, or key, is obvious, please do not ignore it as those who do are likely to get stung.

Point two: clues do not automatically become keys yet often they do. A key is a clue that has been investigated, developed and then with the expanded awareness it brings, may unlock a door or open up lines of further exploration and understanding. When you realize that you have been gifted with a key, any key, it's a '**eureka**' kind of moment, one to savor and enjoy.

To be clear, this N.B.(P.S.) was written solely by the author but of course at Rudy's behest. He appeared to me in a dream last night (12-08-23) to emphasize this thought, an adjunct to the above content. "One of the most important things for you to develop, especially during the 2020's, is your ability to discern." Then he gave me the following example, related to the current holiday season. "Even if you are looking at a sea of seemingly sameness, let's say identical Christmas ornaments, there will still be something to discern, an anomaly perhaps or clue which may then lead to a key. So don't be dazzled by sameness; instead look for the gold, the nugget waiting for your discernment to realize it's there. This is the same as ***voir dire*** *in the legal world except discernment requires questioning yourself rather than a potential juror."*

(Rudy has returned to the driver's seat, is now behind the wheel again.)

Point three: what to do with a key? This I have already alluded to yet it bears repeating. The discovery and then use of a key has the power to change the world. The literal sense of it is to open doors but in any opening of doors new ideas are likely to spill out and make themselves known. Sometimes they are **piccole cose** (*small things*) but they can also be quite important, creating impact or leaving a wake. Think, for example, Edison and Westinghouse, men whose keys opened a number of doors, in their case shedding light far more widely than before. They were 19th century inventors and we continue to live with the effects of their brilliance in the 21st! Did not their work then also have legs?

69

CIRCLES

What's to be said about this, **Signor** Valentino?

One of the most useful of all geometric shapes, you may find circles in many different applications, conceptually and practically.

Starting with the basics, the Sun and the planets that revolve around it essentially are circles, at least from our point of view. And activated blood platelets become circular – by design. That is because it helps them clot so they are an example of a fail-safe mechanism whereas within the blood stream their shape is plate-like, hence the name. Many fruits are round, many flowers too. So, typically, is the face of a clock. One of the most protected places to be is within the confines of a circle. Think traveling in a space capsule or sheltering in a castle, the latter having often been a necessity in times of yore. Circles can deflect arrows and they still do, although today's arrows might be of different stuff from what they once were.

A particularly ubiquitous use of this shape is the wheel, in effect a circle. With it one may achieve continuity of movement as well as traction. Indeed a wheel will never stop turning as long as there is a power source to propel it, mirroring the planets and their relationship with the Sun. A circle can also be thought of as a projection of protection. In séances, also known as mediumistic circles, people tend to sit at a table, preferably a round one. The intent of such a circle, based on intention and prayer, is to create a safe space to effect communication with The Other Side. You (*speaking to the author*) place yourself in such a circle whenever you initiate formal communication with me.

Many design elements are composed of circles or part circles, the quatrefoil, for example, so prevalent in Gothic architecture. Movements of the body too often tend to be circular; think those that are related to the dance. Now let's take this discussion up another notch.

If you will, picture your own life as a circle, one with a beginning and an eventual end which is when the beginning and end unite. Keep in mind, too, that circles can be very elastic just like the length of any incarnation. How to describe this phenomenon? Alpha meets up with Omega on a curved line which will never lack for a horizon. Promise always lies, therefore, just beyond what can be seen. So that is why no one can actually see their end date. The curve in the life trajectory prevents it so all we ever really see is the horizon and with it there is always hope that things continue on indefinitely.

This explains some people believing they will live forever (*in human form*) even when empirical evidence suggests otherwise.

70

BENEFIT/BENEVOLENCE

You (*speaking to the author*) may remember that in addition to what these words mean they are street names in Rhode Island's capital city (*I did not actively remember that but upon checking Rudy is indeed correct.*)

The city I am making reference to is Providence. How curious and yet providential that they appear on the plat and in the vicinity of Brown University, an institution of higher learning. "Providence: the omniscient care of GOD. "This is a city that holds an awareness of its place in the firmament simply by dint of how parts of it have been named. For benefit and benevolence are terms we have lost sight of, words that are all too rarely used in today's world. Instead what you hear is a roar, a clamoring for the 'me' as opposed to the 'we.'

Meanwhile both of these concepts exude a wanting of what's best for all concerned, the most benevolent outcomes. (*M.B.O. is the focus of "The Gentle Way" books, written by Tom T. Moore.*)

Benefit: something that is advantageous or good.

Benevolence: goodwill, charitableness, an act of kindness

Providence is awash in titles that make reference to the common good. The Rhode Island Hospital Trust building is an example of that and it still stands tall, one of the anchors of the business district. If you will, allow a bit of Providence to rub off on you. Indeed, this essay invites you to re-animate the concept of benevolence, the one under which GOD performs each and every one of His/Her miracles. While embracing benevolence is wonderful in and of itself, initiating it is truly the way to go, as much and as often as you can. Consider your actions prior to taking them. Do they have a benevolent flavor? If not, they ought to be reconsidered.

Benevolence slides easily into benefit, benefits plural. A benevolent act is like seeding a field which then has a built-in propensity to flourish and eventually be harvested.

71

THREE STOPS ON THE 24

Transfer Points

(*Those of you who are familiar with San Francisco may recognize that Rudy is referring to a bus line on Divisadero Street.*)

S*peaking to the author.* You make this decision more often than not, to transfer at Geary Blvd, one of the great arteries of the city you often behold.

Let us return to the final observation I made in the essay on circles. Believe it when I said that an 'incarnational' trajectory, also known to you as a lifetime, can be illustrated by a circle, birth being the starting point and death the end. This only happens when the circle is complete and that of course is something we can never know in advance because we cannot see beyond the horizon when a circle is concerned.

There are a few points I really want to hammer in this book and this is one of them. Another is the need to discern, to really hone this skill.

Now take another step. Visualize your life trajectory as at least several circles, typically concentric and in close proximity, which occasionally intersect with each other. Where these intersections occur you will also find transfer points. If you transfer, and very likely you will, you may also transfer back as you see fit. This may be done with alacrity, back and forth, or very deliberately, again up to you, the transferee. Every incarnation has a lot of flexibility and the fact that one can play with timelines to a certain extent supports this contention. Transfer points are usually noticeable because there's often a bit of wobble when you actively engage with a parallel, yet somewhat alternative, lifetime or cycle. That there are typically more than one adds to the dynamism which of course is what any incarnation is all about, is it not?

Let us hope none of this is in any way surprising, stipulating that you may have not previously thought about your current incarnation within the context of this terminology and its associated glimmers. For here I am only offering you a glimpse of the way things work, incarnational multiplicities and how they spark each other. As I have previously stated, no one lives their life in a straight line; it is curved and varied at best and rarely is there ever only one course of action or circle of life from which to choose.

In a practical sense a transfer point may also be noticed when someone suddenly chooses a completely different life style: a city dweller moving to the country, let's say, or a dramatic change of profession or relationship status. Such actions are often ascribed to a shift in perspective on the part of the individual in question. It is also a clue that a transfer point has been activated. Speaking for myself I negotiated quite a few, some of which were noticeable in my personal life plus others in my career.

72

FLUIDITY

In the physical world this is easily illustrated by the human body, its constant circulation of blood and the cycle of liquid consumed being commensurate with liquid excreted. One could therefore say that fluids form the basis of our very being, are intrinsic to existence in human form. And fluids also express interdependency and connectivity, requirements that make animation possible.

Where I reside things are similar but instead of physical fluids being involved, think rays of Light which are the sole basis for the animating principle inherent in all non-corporeal entities, including, of course, **moi**. They create cosmic fluidity and more or less operate in the same way as do bodily functions. So it is safe to say that is how life is eternally maintained, in the body or not.

Being in the Earth Plane requires feeling comfortable with issues of fluidity for a large portion of what is perceived as Earth's surface is covered by water. And most of you will have been 'at sea' at one time or another, pun intended, where the waters can sometimes be turbulent.

And what about the fluidity you may have need of, for the balance of this decade and beyond? There is a French verb, **se faufiler**, whose English equivalent is to slip or squeeze through and its inclusion here is both to be instructive and the source of a potential strategy.

'Obstacular' - the flavor of our times and another word I've coined to make a point!

And so what is the best mindset for dealing with obstacles? Think water, fluids, fluidity! In any successful 'squeeze-through' there will be a discernible lack of friction.

73

POWER DIFFERENTIALS

Bullying

These things cannot be ignored on the Earth Plane for if you do you do so at your own peril. This is a global phenomenon so I will not attempt to ascribe it to any particular country or part of the world. From a macro point of view, the fact that it exists is simply an example of contrast, the mother's milk of discernment.

Society in general is stratified, layers upon layers, and at the same time all of the layers interact and commingle.

That said, occasionally a jackal makes itself known, usually in the form of a would-be strongman or dictator, someone to whom large swaths of population want to entrust their power as if they are not capable of wielding it themselves. The idea is that the person presenting as dictator can solve all of their problems which of course is rubbish. Then, due to any number of factors, a myth is born and a portion of the populace descends into a state of mass hypnosis, slavishly worshiping said dictator.

Inherent in any dictator personality profile is their penchant to bully other people to get their way, and/or use bullying as a cudgel to expand their power. Other traits one might see in a dictator: a propensity to the maniacal, the devious, the uttering of falsehoods, all in service of their own ends.

What is the basis for any citizenry to want to lend themselves to such an enterprise, dictator-date, if you will? First and foremost it is fear - but fear of what exactly? They would often not be able to tell you so I will: you must fear "the other," namely any segments of society the dictator chooses to demonize, for whatever reason.

Notice I am not naming names. You have only to think about the past century and the present one to create a list ("If the shoe fits, wear it.")

74

CASTAGNE

(*Chestnuts*)

Considered a delicacy most everywhere except in the United States, chestnuts rule the fall because that is when they become seasonally available. Have any of you ever bought a bag of hot chestnuts or eaten **crème aux marrons** while traveling in France? Hopefully so because if not you most certainly will have missed out on a lovely taste treat.

Here, however, we are going to focus on "old chestnuts" which have nothing to do with the foodstuff just referenced.

Old Chestnut: a joke or story that has become tedious because of its age and constant repetition.

The challenge is being able to recognize when old chestnuts are flung in your direction, as opposed to clear, concise ideas or concepts. Too often repetition is our foe because propaganda in any form has the effect of dulling one's senses. The political class adores old chestnuts, first because they sound familiar to those hearing them and second because the emotions they elicit may be useful to induce certain citizenry to vote for specific candidates.

Old chestnuts are akin to buzzwords and buzz phrases that have already been worked to death. Take for example the phrase 'witch hunt' for it tickles the ivories of an old tune going back to medieval times when so-called witches actually were being pursued, whereas if you stop to think about it such imagery has no relevance in today's world.

Old Chestnuts may also be thought of as clichés, so overused for sure and probably hackneyed as well. I have mentioned politicians and their love for this device but we should not forget the world of advertising, the hard sell, which often draws water from the same well.

Mes amis, some of you are walking around with old chestnuts seared into your brains. If so, now is the time to perform a little surgery.

75

I AM STATEMENTS

The most important declarations one ever makes for not only do such statements help create your reality they support and reinforce it.

The following is an excerpt from "Valentino Speaks" ©2011, included here at Rudy's request.

"The power of I AM is not always properly recognized or sometimes even acknowledged. Whereas "I AM" is the most powerful statement in the Universe.

The Creator said, says and will say I AM as a constant. Each I AM intersects and loops into the next, creating an energetic chain and thereby forming the multi-dimensional canvas of the All That Is. The never ending declaration I AM creates WHAT IS. There is never a time or a space when the Creator's I AM is not. Such reverberations are the stuff of the Universe. I am using the term Universe here in order to attempt to concretize the vastness that is the ALL IN ALL so that it might be better understood.

Soul Entities are the channels through which the Creator's I AM is differentiated into form. Therefore, it is a given that we, as reflections of the Creator, also frequently declare I AM. However, we sometimes have gaps in the continuity of our statements or we may choose unproductive wording. Ah yes, here's one of the rubs of incarnation. Be careful how you program your I AM statements. Do note the frequency and consistency of what you say. To create constructive outcomes, I AM statements have to be constructive. They must also be firmly anchored on the 'stage' by no dearth of repetition. Therefore, be consistent and positive, as well as relatively frequent, as you declare yourself to be who you are.

The personality often wants to insert words into our I AM statements that express temporary frustration, low self esteem or facets of what some might call image management. However, do not go there. Be aware of how the things you say affect your life. What you say, both to yourself and others, creates an ongoing, ever-manifesting network of events exactly mirroring the tenor and import of your words. Words have power. In fact, they are power ~ in encapsulated form. Choose them assiduously, avoiding verbal pitfalls. Create what you truly want to create by knowing that your thoughts and words are continually imaging the reality you experience on a daily basis.

To truly be all that you can, you must, as much as is possible, verbalize what is creative and most powerfully constructive. By choosing to know that only good reigns, it will. This is what is known as the power of positive thinking. Its virtues have been extolled by many people, from Mary Baker Eddy in my lifetime to Wayne Dyer in yours."

76

LIVING VICARIOUSLY

Vlogging is a relatively recent phenomenon, at least in terms of the intensity with which it is being practiced at the present time. And some of you are immersed in it, either by enthusiastically watching vlogs or creating your own.

Vlog topics can be as numerous as grains of sand on a beach but they usually involve 'doing something' - for example, home renovation. And they may also detail other activities like travel or shopping. Watching vlogs is a way to drop into other people's lives without making a commitment to actually getting involved with them, but of course you always do have the option of supporting your favorite vloggers via monetary donations. That, too, seems to be rather prevalent these days and it is how some of them fund their projects and lifestyles.

None of this is necessarily a problem yet here is the core question, the one each and every one of you must pose to yourself: to what extent do I want to live my life vicariously? How does this serve me and when does it not?

Of course everyone lives vicariously to some degree. That is a given. The moment you open a novel you automatically begin to observe the characters it contains as well as their motivations. The same is true when you watch a film. That said, never abrogate your own life, what you must do for yourself, in service of being fixated on the lives of others. Sure, we learn plenty from observation but what sticks the most, what is most assimilated, is always what you actually do, the skills you develop, the understandings that you have come to of your own accord.

Vloggers may show you how to demolish a wall or paper a room but then you have to do it yourself to really understand what is truly involved.

77

INTENTIONS

"Yet if they waffle, they get little more than butter and syrup" - Shawn Schikora

Questions: Is it advisable to state our intentions without attaching specifics? Do qualifiers limit our possibilities? If one is too steeped in their intentions, might they be ignoring issues they really should heed?

There is an art to intention and best practice, I would say, means keeping them simple, direct, and most of all easily-stated. A short sentence should suffice rather than any sort of treatise. The Universe hears better in such cases as any hint of confusion will have been eliminated by your having honed your intention prior to initializing it. And simplicity also makes it easier for you to repeat it. Yes, state your intention (s) aloud whenever you have the opportunity. Sound is an anchor, a magnifier as well. Then of course keep any and all intentions front and center in your mind chatter too. And once an intention has been crafted be open to refining it as the circumstances around you change.

Intentions should never be chiseled in stone for flexibility is crucial to their unfurling in a way that is commensurate with your master plan, whatever that may be.

We could also think of our intentions as propellants for if we had none we would likely be adrift and subject to the whims of others, playing parts in their intentions rather than fostering our own. It should be noted, however, that we do often help others achieve their intentions but that only works well when we also have some. How much fun is it, by the way, to encounter someone who has parallel intentions ~ not congruent but in the same ballpark? Think about that.

Your interlocutor wonders if GOD sometimes practices tough love where intentions are concerned. No, I would say you practice tough love with yourself as your intentions may not always fully align with the needs and wants of your soul. In such cases reverses or static may be encountered and if you find blockages on your intentional byways it is always a good idea to reassess, by deletion or refinement, that particular intention.

78

GUIDANCE

You are, of course, your own guide in everything you say and do, and a damn good one at that. Intelligence is inherent in your being and on the day you were born, you came in with a massive pool of experience and knowledge to draw upon.

And then you also have a spirit guide, a wise one who is always in your corner and not only, because other spirit guides also assist from time to time in helping to keep you whole for the length of your incarnation. All of the beings so involved are, without a doubt, Masters and Teachers of the highest realms.

Bottom line, aren't you lucky? You can make choices completely of your own volition, using your own resources, and/or you may also choose to consult with spirit through prayer or a simple request. Know that when you get stumped you can always ask for help in terms of the best pathway forward. And rest assured answers will be forthcoming, often perceived in flashes or pulse-like understandings, **relámpagos** they say in Spanish (*bolts of lightning.*)

Guidance always involves walking a tightrope. Of course, initiate as many decisions as you can on your own but at the same time never hesitate to call upon your guides whenever they are needed, especially if you feel hamstrung. They have been assigned to you for a reason and their support is not a one way street; your experiences are teaching them just as they are teaching you so one could say it is a mutually beneficial association.

In wending your way around the Earth Plane, never think yourself alone because that is just not ever the case. Spirit friends abound even when physical ones lack and of course it is always nice for us to have both.

79

GRATITUDE

The most healing lubricant the world has ever known: that is my summation of the attitude of gratitude.

Picture yourself surrounded by cogs such as those found inside an old-fashioned clock mechanism, in this case a euphemism for the complexities of an incarnational cycle. Being grateful is what supports your maintenance, the smooth functioning of said mechanism and, concurrently, the fewest number of visits to a repair shop. If you are grateful every day, for both the smaller and larger happenings in your life, you will have enhanced your shine, the Light you emit by dint of being a Soul. And the glow resulting from your expressions of gratitude will have the effect of attracting more abundance into your life, more beneficence, more benevolent outcomes.

Expressing gratitude creates a circle of perpetual generation. The more grateful you are, the more blessings you shall encounter. And the more blessings you encounter, the more grateful you will be. So, **mes amis**, if you haven't already done so please do actualize this, one of the loveliest of all metaphysical principles.

An important thing to remember about any incarnation is that 'your cup runneth over' and all you have to do to make it so is to start priming the pump.

80

CELEBRATION

We have a lot to celebrate and in saying we, I mean you and I, (*speaking to the author*) because there were a few "sliding on ice" moments in the preparation and development of this book. Nevertheless they were overcome, strategies tried and perfected, the net result of which is that we were both empowered by the experience.

And so it is. No project is completely devoid of trip wires from inception to completion. Happy to say that in our case there were only a few and that they were easily expedited!

Now what about this topic? What to celebrate and why? The answer is everything (for what) and just because (for why.) We do not celebrate enough, for you could easily find multiple reasons to do so on a daily basis. Celebration is an outcome, also a corollary, of gratitude. They go together. We often think in terms of holidays which we then associate with celebrations whereas every day's a holiday if you want it to be. Celebrate the dawn of a new day, for example, or your first swim of the summer season. Anything may inspire you to celebrate and so it should.

(*Speaking to the author*) Today (*1-5-24*) you watched a video in which the entity known as Alcazar made this recommendation: "move into the center of your being-ness."

If you can do this, and you can, it will be a celebratory moment for the whole of mankind. And the more frequently you do this, the quicker we become immersed in the Aquarian way as advocates for oneness as opposed to dualities. So you may say, "Rudy, why do you quote another source here?" Because I am not the sole purveyor of truth and neither are you. Truth is where you find it and if relevant it should always be acknowledged.

Again, anything that can be celebrated should be and all that is needed to make it happen is the accompanying thought - no gifts, special meals or specific festivities required!

AFTERWORD

1

WVH

Why me? What are the qualifications that I possess and how are they aligned with the energies of the non-corporeal entity known to us as Rudolph Valentino?

Alignment is the key word here and that, essentially, is the basis for our having co-created a total of six books, this one likely to be the last.

As has been mentioned previously, Rudy and I have encountered each other while inhabiting other bodies, times, and places. So the fact that we have been working together for approximately twenty years in this life should not be too surprising because we have worked together before. This time the work is about being of service, shedding light, and opening minds. And on a more personal level it is also about cooperation and respect, about refining those particular aspects of self through the medium of automatic writing, the process we used to create the contents of our books.

There are of course lots of other correlations. For example, I have spoken and written knowledge of four of the languages Rudy routinely used during his 31 year lifetime: Italian, French, Spanish, and of course English. That is why he often inserts words or phrases from the first three into the material being received. He knows I won't have to run to a dictionary to decipher them although sometimes I do, and that is when he presents me with something completely new which, when I look it up, is always perfect for whatever he is wanting to convey.

Rudy's astrological chart and mine blend together quite harmoniously. Therefore the language of astrology also supports our respective and mutual alignment which is the requisite for our ability to communicate with each other. In the chart comparison there are factors that speak to our having, and having had, a strong connection.

Though I am choosing not to reveal all of the reasons for our book-writing projects I do hope that I will have given you a sense of why they occurred.

Collaborating with Rodolfo has been one of the most delightful experiences of my life. We hope that you have enjoyed reading our books as much as we have enjoyed writing them!

***Vi auguriamo il meglio del meglio, adesso e sempre*!** (*We wish you the best of the best, now and always!*)

Wayne Vincent Hatford
San Francisco, California

AFTERWORD

2

RVG

Six; this is the sum of our collaborations, the number of books we have created, including the one you have just finished reading.

Consider, if you will, the number 6 purely from a numerological point of view. There is a **benessere** (*sense of well-being*) about it, also an impulse to be of service. And this is what we ultimately grasped and brought to fruition. Notice the use of grasp for that is what Wayne had to do to effectuate our work, grasp a pen and put it to paper while allowing me the use of his energy field for specific amounts of time. The ensuing automatic writing sessions, which for this book numbered eighty plus, gave me the opportunity to catapult my thoughts across dimensional lines. As you may imagine this was, by definition, a heady experience. I was the information source and Wayne did all the leg work, including the tasks directly related to book publication.

You may wonder what set the stage for us to become metaphysical intimates. We were cousins once in Ancient Egypt reconnoitering along the Nile by torchlight. In 9th century Arabia we traded camels for a living and later perished together in a sandstorm. And in medieval Italy we knew each other as competitors, gunpowder experts whose experimentations ended in mutual disaster. There have also been other times and places where we have interacted but the ones I cite here give you a sense of the scope and depth of our synergy.

And in being of service with the content of our books, what were we looking to accomplish, individually and as a duo? Balance, cooperation, also convention. The first two are self-explanatory and the third was about making an agreement and then sticking to it. At the beginning of this journey neither of us knew how many books would be forthcoming. Nevertheless we made a commitment to work together to produce them and indeed we have done so!

Here you have two points of Light, each a whirling dervish, who looked across the Universe and perceived each other's beings. **Grazie di cuore**, Wayne, (*my heart-felt thanks*) and to all who chose to read our books, **mes remerciements éternels** (*my eternal thanks*!) May your personal 'shines' become ever more brighter!

Con affetto,
(*With affection*)

Rodolfo Valentino Guglielmi

Made in the USA
Coppell, TX
29 March 2024

30671840R00115